Movie Speak

How to Talk Like You Belong on a Film Set

and get invited to the four-banger.

BY TONY BILL

WORKMAN PUBLISHING • NEW YORK

Library of Congress Cataloging-in-Publication Data is available.

ISBN 978-0-7611-4359-8

Workman books are available at special discounts when purchased
in bulk for premiums and sales promotions as well as for fund-
raising or educational use. Special editions or book excerpts also
can be created to specification. For details, contact the Special Sales
Director at the address below.

Cover design by David Matt
Design by David Matt and Gary Montalvo
Illustrations by Katie Maratta and Peter Maratta

WORKMAN PUBLISHING COMPANY, INC.
225 Varick Street
New York, NY 10014-4381
workman.com

Printed in U.S.A.
First printing December 2008

10 9 8 7 6 5 4 3

CONTENTS

Introduction
Lights! Camera! Diction!

A LITTLE OVER a hundred years ago, in 1895, a couple of guys who spoke only French invented the movies. Two brothers named Louis and Auguste Lumière forever changed the way pictures were looked at. It happened in a small, dark basement in Paris, where some thirty-five people had been attracted by a sign on the street that read "Lumière Cinématographe." No one in the room had any idea of what was about to take place. When the lights went down and the screen started to flicker, the people were astounded. They'd never seen anything like it.

A dozen years later, in 1907, a film crew stepped off a train in downtown Los Angeles. These invaders consisted of Francis Boggs, the director, and Thomas Persons, who was the cameraman, propman, business manager, assistant director, and whatever else was required. They had already shot the interiors of their film in Chicago. Now, despite the minor technicality of an entire change of cast, they were to film the rest of it in California. A year later, they finished it—a full reel, all one thousand feet of it: *The Count of Monte Cristo.* It was the first big California feature, and following its debut, Boggs and Persons set up a studio on a rooftop on Main Street in downtown Los Angeles.

History does not record the way Louis and Auguste or Francis and Thomas spoke on their first sets, but soon they began to invent, discover, or stumble across a way to express themselves on a film set that no one else had imagined.

Movie sets are another country with a language all their own, much of it rich in history, much of it fading or forgotten. There are virtually no written records of the etymology of many of these words and expressions. It's a largely oral tradition passed down over the last hundred years. Old-timers and "experts," crew members and scholars, all depend on an unwritten record from whence many of these terms derive. But the language prevails. Just as with the nautical or aeronautical lexicon, it's the only *accepted* way of communicating. So this is a book about that and other aspects of the movie life. As much as possible, I include not just what *I* know about making movies, but also what everybody else knows about making movies; what everybody knows but won't quite admit; what everybody knows but didn't know they knew. An insider's book for outsiders.

To be sure, there is an endless supply of nomenclature, slang, and colorful expressions on a movie set. Many words are technical, some are odd but self-explanatory, and many have become familiar enough to the general public to need no definition. I've tried here to present the most colorful, mysterious, and useful of the bunch: the ones that can get you through any day with plenty left over for the next.

It seems that everyone these days wants to make movies. Whether it be as a writer, actor, director, producer, cinematographer, or other crewmember, they all yearn to join this not-so-secret society; to learn its ways, its coded rules, and its language. The only trouble is, you have to be a member before you can learn—and you have to learn before you can be a member. If you walk onto a set, you have to talk the talk. You can't (or shouldn't) direct a movie and tell the crew to "Move that little thingamajig a little bit that way, and shoot kind of a close shot of the actor from about waist up so I can see him when the extra walks by, and move the camera a little bit that way."

Instead, you'd say something like, "Give me two Ts or a cowboy with the Jack Lord and make sure the B.G. is visible as you pan. And maybe we'll make that a one-er, so just banana left."

Confused? I hope you won't be for long.

To my wife,
Helen Bartlett,
who produces fine movies, beautiful daughters . . .
and all the best years of my life.

And to Francesca,
Maddie, *and* Daphne.

Abby Singer, The Normally referred to simply as **the Abby,** this is always the second-to-last shot of the day. Named for the eponymous production manager/producer who, as an **assistant director (A.D.)** in the early days of television, realized that a few extra shots could be squeezed out of the day's schedule if the crew began packing up and moving to the next location *before* a location move took place. Over the course of a day, this could save up to an hour of shooting time. This penchant for hustle and efficiency earned Singer a place in crews' hearts and film's history, and coined the phrase now heard 'round the world and understood in many languages.

The eagerly anticipated announcement of the Abby is always accompanied by at least mild rejoicing among the crew. It is best first revealed sotto voce by the director to the A.D., whose privilege it should be to announce it.

One caveat: A director can avoid embarrassment by making *absolutely sure* that the penultimate shot is indeed at hand before he confirms the Abby Singer, for if he reneges more than once or twice during a given production, it will be cause for behind-the-back mockery, if not open distrust. It is tantamount to lying to children or taking away their candy.

above-the-line items

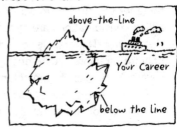

Above-the-line

Elements of the budget that normally include only the salaries of the star(s), director, producer, writer, and underlying literary rights. The rest of the budget items—crew, locations, music, film, editing, etc., are **below-the-line items.** The "line" is the line on the page of the budget that separates the two categories. Above- and below-the-line personnel are also often referred to as a group, sort of like the way people talk about the rich folks and the poor folks.

action! The universal director's command, though some opt for a customized signal such as "Okay," "Go," or a simple nod of the head. (Samuel Fuller carried a Luger that he would fire sometimes in lieu of yelling "Action!" Martin Scorsese often says, "Action. Energy!" And Clint Eastwood just says—softly, of course—"Go ahead" or, perhaps as a nod to his Sergio Leone roots, *"Actione."*)

Contrary to public perception, it is not always the director who "calls the action," as the saying goes. Some directors leave it to the A.D., which accomplishes a couple of things: First, it ensures that the person responsible for all the departments is aware and ready for the shot to begin. (And a good A.D. will be able to read a director's mind, often eliminating the need to even ask when to call the action.) Second, it's simply one less thing for the director to worry about at a moment when a zillion considerations are already on his/her mind.

Warning: This transfer of authority is recommended only for directors secure enough to relinquish one of the several trappings of omnipotence that attach to the job.

For a hundred years or so, actors have had to perform on this sort of command. But with the digital revolution, it is less necessary to divide the day into "shooting" time and "rehearsal" time. Equally unnecessary is the order to "cut." I think this presages a revolution in acting and directing, akin to the influence of Method acting fifty or so years ago (*see also* The Death of Acting, page 10).

A.D. Assistant Director. The A.D. is to the director as copilot is to pilot, as bos'n is to skipper, as Sancho Panza is to Don Quixote. As with all other jobs on the set—including such formerly male-dominated bastions as **transpo** captain, **wrangler, grip, D.P.,** and, of course, **director,** the A.D. may be female as easily as male. Well, almost as easily.

In addition to the first A.D., there is a second A.D. Then, depending on how many extras, cars, cameras, animals, etc., are employed on a given day, there is a *second* second, then an *additional* second. After that, the duties are usually covered by a production assistant

(**P.A.**). The hierarchy does not accommodate naming third and fourth A.D.s.

A.D.R. Automated Dialogue Replacement. Formerly (and still) called **looping,** this is the standard method of digitally rerecording an actor's dialogue to replace lines that need to be changed. The two usual reasons are lack of acceptable quality of the production sound track (airplanes overhead, extraneous noise on the set, etc.) or "protection" of objectionable language for versions to be used for network television and airline viewing.

adjustment A **bump** in pay given to a stuntperson for performing a particularly complex or dangerous stunt. Adjustments are somewhat subjective, often negotiated, and can sometimes be given to other crewmembers; for example, when a camera crew is placed in a potentially dangerous location to film a stunt. Principal actors and directors, because they are on a flat fee, never get adjustments.

Alan Smithee A pseudonym used by DGA (Directors Guild of America) directors who want their credit removed from a film. To use this name, the director must prove to the Guild that the film has been taken from his or her creative control. The director is also required to keep the reason for the disavowal a secret. Obviously, this protection is not offered on non-DGA films.

The practice began with *Death of a Gunfighter* in 1969. The star, Richard Widmark, and the director,

Robert Totten, had what is usually euphemistically called "creative differences." Guess who prevailed? Totten was replaced by Don Siegel, but neither director wanted to be identified with the finished film. So it was credited to "Al Smith"—until they realized there was already an actual Al Smith in the DGA. So they came up with Alan Smithee, which interestingly anagrammatizes into "The Alias Men."

The DGA discontinued the Alan Smithee practice—ironically, in part due to a 1997 film called *An Alan Smithee Film: Burn Hollywood Burn,* which was so fraught with real-life creative drama that the film's director, Arthur Hiller, actually asked for an Alan Smithee credit—but the pseudonym's place in film and TV history is well entrenched.

And he may return someday. In 1998, director Tony Kaye clashed with Edward Norton over the editing of *American History X.* Kaye took out ads attacking the film and tried to be credited as "Humpty Dumpty." The DGA refused his request.

anamorphic A wide-screen format with an aspect ratio of 2.39:1, meaning the picture width is 2.39 times its height. Also known as *scope,* deriving from CinemaScope, the Twentieth Century Fox technology introduced in 1952.

answer print The first version of a film that is printed after the sound has been synced. The print is intended to "answer" a director's concerns about color correction and sound and optical timing. Once the answer print (or first final proof) has been approved, other prints can be made.

apple box Along with the **C47** and the **mouse,** one of the last useful vestiges of the kind of set where the producer produced, the actors acted, and the crew wore ties. Nominally, apple boxes come in three sizes: full, half, and quarter. Very often referred to without using the word "box": simply apple. Also among the last handmade tools of the trade, their uses are limitless: I use a personal apple to sit on instead of a **director's chair;** it doesn't require a Sherpa and it lacks pretension.

Apple Box

1st position   2nd position   3rd position   Really tricky position

Technical Note: The industry standard measurements of the full apple box are: 8" × 12" × 20". Also there are three positions possible: #1, flat; #2, on edge; #3, on end. There's an even better set of designations: Placed upright in its tallest position, it's known as "New York"; laid down flat, it's "Texas"; on its side, it's "California." Only really cool crewmembers know this.

arm up To raise the arm of a crane. Arm down, of course, you can figure out for yourself.

armorer Anytime a firearm is to be used on the set, an armorer is required to be present (or should be). Responsible for providing or securing the guns, loading the blanks, and instructing the actors in their use. (On movie sets, blanks are not called blanks. They are referred to by their power: quarter loads, half loads, three-quarter loads, and—occasionally—full loads.) The sound you hear in the theater is always added in postproduction.

Arri An Arriflex camera. Comes in 16, 35, and 65/70 mm formats, as well as digital. The cool thing to know about this word is the origin of the name: It derives from the names of the founders of the ARRI company in Munich in 1917, August **Ar**nold and Robert **Ri**chter. (*See also* **handheld.**)

associate producer The bottom rung of the producer credit ladder, yet often the most intimately involved, hardworking, and contributive of the lot. Here's an interesting test: Ask the **executive producer, producer, coproducer,** and associate producer to name the members of the crew. Keep score.

In feature films, the "produced by" credit is the Holy Grail; the Academy Award is given to the producer(s) of the best picture. Nowadays, the credit has been considerably debased and devalued by the ploy of using it as a sop to powerful actors, writers, and directors or in exchange for money or other favors . . . or just to make them feel good. The Producer's Guild of America (PGA) has struggled to curb this enthusiasm, and influenced the Academy of Motion Picture Arts and Sciences (AMPAS) to follow its lead, by limiting the number of producers to be credited. (It's unlikely that this issue will be permanently resolved.)

The great director Billy Wilder once remarked, "Were the associate producers the only ones willing to associate with the producers?" A more telling description, equally uncharitable, is a line from David Mamet's 2000 film *State and Main.* Asked "What's an associate producer credit?" a character replies, "It's what you give your secretary instead of a raise."

In television, the king of the credit mountain is the executive producer. That's who gets the **Emmy.**

Note: It is impossible to determine the actual function, power, talent, or creative contribution of a producer based on any of the aforementioned credits, including, these days, the possessive credit ("A Joe Blow Film" or "A Film by Joe Blow"). It is equally unreliable to query the director, the writer, or any studio executive or crewmember. The producer, of course, may be expected to be utterly self-serving in remembering individual contributions. In the case of hit films, this means that no one will ever accurately describe or remember who did what. In the case of failed films, these "memories" will tend to be affected by the often-predictable case of résumé amnesia. The old adage "Success has many fathers, but failure is an orphan" always applies here.

"The art of acting is not to act; once you show them more, what you show them, in fact, is bad acting."
—SIR ANTHONY HOPKINS

The Death of Acting

EVERYBODY KNOWS by now that the digital revolution is upon us, that you can make a real movie with a couple of crewmembers and a home-video camera *(Once, The Blair Witch Project, Pieces of April)*. But there's an equally exciting, though little-mentioned, effect of that technology. I'm going to break the rules of good dramatic writing and give away my point right now: Screen acting as we know it is terminally ill and ready to die. A new form of performance is about to take its place, and you don't need to sign up for lessons. It'll happen without your knowing it—as inevitably and suddenly and relentlessly as it happened in the mid-1920s with the introduction of sound. It happened once again in the fifties, when Marlon Brando, James Dean, Paul Newman, Kim Stanley, Geraldine Page, and many others popularized the Method.

And, like all deaths, it will presage a rebirth.

I am, I will confess, a born-again digital user. I have renounced the satanic tyranny of film and embraced the new director's god of the twenty-first century: "digital capture." It happened quickly and recently: In 2004, I directed *Flyboys,* a story of the first combat pilots; young American boys who volunteered to fly for France in World War I. We shot it in fifty days. Well, we shot the actors in fifty days; the airplanes took a little bit longer. The special effects took longer still—but those are other stories. Let's stick with the actors.

Like all screen actors who have appeared in front of the camera since film and sprockets and cameras were combined with lights and directors and other actors—and any number of animals, vehicles, and props—our actors learned their lines, rehearsed their actions, and then launched into their performances as the director, yours truly, called "action" and the camera rolled. Except for one big difference: *There was no film in the camera.*

The camera we used, the Panavision Genesis, was the first 35 mm digital camera—one generation beyond high-definition video. It uses the Panavision lenses currently in the front of hundreds of 35 mm film cameras around the world, the standard system of recording the "reality" of the actors who perform before it. Aptly named, it was the first of its breed: It records on a tiny digital cassette for forty minutes between instant "reloads," it records in light levels that are considerably below those necessary for film, it makes no sound. And it represents the end of an era, a revolution. It is to cameras as sprockets were to film. A few years later, there are now several other cameras of similar quality and lesser cost available. There is, save for ignorance and inertia, no turning back.

No film in the camera. Digital shooting completely eliminates the need to watch dailies, to "check the gate" for dirt, scratches, or imperfections, to wonder if a stunt really worked or a magical moment was captured. Was that something in the background we didn't see? Was that extra looking in the lens? No problem. There is nothing to send to the lab or to watch the next day—or even later. *No film* purchased, exposed, developed, wasted, or printed. There is no production time lost—easily worth a half hour a day—to reload and check the camera (in all our many days I never noticed a "reload"). There are no short ends to deal with; no questions about what was seen on camera during a take. What you saw—on a high-resolution, big-screen monitor—is what you got. And *no dailies:* Another hour, at least, saved in the director's waking, working day.

> There is, save for ignorance and inertia, no turning back.

The final image, whether projected digitally (a burgeoning technology in theaters: Currently there are several thousand so equipped in the U.S., and inevitably all will be digital) or on 35 mm film, as it is currently projected, is indistinguishable from an original 35 mm image—in fact, arguably it is superior. But there are several other superior aspects. Among them: It never wears out (digitally projected, there are no scratches, breaks, or damages) and there is no extra expense transferring it to the now-ubiquitous "digital intermediate"—a savings of several hundreds of thousands of dollars.

I should also add that despite the fact that we were driving the Model T of the new technology on *Flyboys*, we had not a moment of downtime due to technical problems. In fact, almost perversely, we had no Panavision or video technician on the set. Our cameraman, Henry Braham, had no experience with this camera, yet we lost not a minute to relighting, reshooting, or second-guessing. Bright daylight exteriors, aerial dogfight sequences, day-for-night scenes, nighttime scenes—all were shot convincingly and quickly, and were qualitatively superior to film.

Also superior to film is the latitude of exposure and the adaptability to digital effects. Operating temperatures are considerably expanded, and there is no sound of running film to dampen or eliminate in the case of very close shots. There was, in short, no aspect aesthetically or financially inferior to shooting on film. Rather, there was an enormous saving in time and money and convenience, with no trade-off in quality. But that's the least of it. What's most exciting about it, to me, is what this new technology really represents and where it inevitably will lead the artists in front of the camera.

For a hundred years actors have performed in front of cameras, struggling to create, or re-create, reality. And for a hundred years they have carried a secret burden: the burden of using up money by the second. When the camera is rolling, film—an expensive, fragile, rather unpredictable strip of chemicals—has been racing through the shutter at ninety feet a minute and, after all is shot and done, about $5,500 an hour per camera. An hour of digital tape, by contrast, costs about $135.

Beyond that, during rehearsals—the actor's one chance to experiment, fail, improvise, stumble, or fall—the camera *isn't* rolling; it would normally be a very expensive waste of film. But then the set is silenced, dozens of crew scurry into invisibility, the camera crew is alerted, and the call of "Rolling!" signals the start of filming, with a ritualistic intensity that culminates in the cry of "Action!" And, for the poor actor, the pressure is on: the pressure to not waste film, to not use up precious resources, the pressure—an actor's worst enemy—*to be good*. To not screw it up. To be fresh. To be surprising. To be real. To get it right. Often in one take. Above all, *not to act*.

But it's never like the rehearsal, when the camera isn't rolling, when precious film isn't being "wasted." Somewhere on the set is a producer or production manager—and somewhere in every actor's consciousness there is a monitor—counting the footage, adding up the vast expense of the exposed, developed, and printed footage. Every actor knows what it's like to give their best performance in the rehearsal only to spend, often in vain, the rest of the allotted time trying to recapture that magic. And every director knows the frustration of trying to coax an actor into doing what they did in rehearsal, when they were relaxed and un-self-conscious. But now, with digital, there is *no more rehearsal*. No difference between rehearsal and performance, because rehearsal *is* performance. And in time it will

> But now, with digital, there is *no more rehearsal*. No difference between rehearsal and performance, because rehearsal *is* performance.

be obvious that performance is no different than rehearsal. You can forget your lines, trip over the furniture, improvise, and miss your marks. If the camera was on the set, the performance will be on the screen. This, by the way, is good for at least another free half hour in the shooting day.

For years one of the highest praises visited upon an actor's performance has been that they were acting "as if the camera weren't there." In fact, this is often the public's most indelible impression of acting skill. But it's a completely false one. For any middling actor, there's virtually nothing intimidating about a camera being on the set; after all, "real life" occurs in front of all sorts of appurtenances: cars, lamps, pedestrians, neighbors, etc. The camera is just another movable piece of equipment on the set. *Until it starts rolling.* That's when it gets intimidating. That's when people make all those mistakes and waste all that film.

Point an unloaded camera at someone, then tell them it's rolling. It's the difference between pointing a toy gun at someone and then aiming one with bullets in it.

The film camera isn't the actor's enemy. It's just an antiquated nineteenth-century box of shutters and gears. The *film* that's coursing through it is the enemy. The whole trick of directing and acting in fictional films—and the biggest challenge of making documentaries—is to make the subjects *unaware that the camera's rolling.* That's why rehearsals are so easy for actors, why their off-camera performances are usually so much more natural and relaxed than when they're on-camera. All over Los Angeles and New York, actors are in "film-acting" or "audition" classes, studying, all to one end: how to ignore the camera. Now the camera will ignore *them.*

Meanwhile, every actor secretly dreads the surprise announcement of "Reload!" as the crews' eyes roll up and the director's roll down and their fellow actors' eyes turn somewhere away. Then they have to get themselves back together to start again or—worse for many actors—pick up where they left off. In particularly emotional scenes, actors often never quite get back to their pre-reload intensity. (Of course, it can be argued that the pressure imposed by the running camera leads to an intensity and concentration that mere rehearsal cannot accomplish, but not many actors would agree with that claim. I'd submit that there's certainly enough pressure to perform without that added by the celluloid whizzing through the camera.)

Along with that breakthrough comes the dissolution of most of an actor's fears: flubbing a line, sneezing—any number of perceived accidents—and having the director cut and start again. (But not, often, before a discussion as to whether there's enough film left in the camera to make it worthwhile, or should we throw away what's left and take a few minutes to reload? And why don't you just go sit down while we reset and reload and take it easy and try to get back into your performance after that?) All these dreaded moments—and the days and nights filled with them— are now over.

I envision subtle but noticeable changes in the job of the director and camera operator as well. As mentioned, rehearsal is now an obsolete concept. So, apart from blocking the scene, why rehearse?

> ## All these dreaded moments...are now over.

Lars von Trier's *Breaking the Waves* ushered in an interesting approach to shooting a scene: Two camera operators simply stepped into the scene and started shooting away. If they saw each other, they cut it out in editing, but for the most part they simultaneously and continuously shot the whole scene, from beginning to end, not stopping to reset the actors, to reload the cameras, or to accommodate new angles: no regard for screen direction. In short, a revolution in filmmaking technique—and a revolution for the actors, who were free to move anywhere on the set or within the rooms where the scenes took place: total liberation from hitting marks, being conscious of lighting, or repeating rehearsed action.

There's another area due for a complete rethink: the whole concept of long-shot, two-shot single, etc. With digital, a two-shot can yield one or two singles *in the editing room*. Why waste time on the set when you can shoot a one-size-fits-all on the set . . . especially under extreme time constraints? A close-up can be noisy; actors are often conscious of the film running through the sprockets. It can be intimidating. Film can be blown up about 15 percent before it starts to lose quality and become grainy; the Genesis image can be blown up 200 percent or more. You can pan, dolly, zoom in or out in the editing room, too. This ability is bound to change how a director chooses to budget the shooting day, and, once again, will impact the actors. The actors used to know what the shot was—close, medium, long—and would often adjust their performances accordingly. This could be good . . . but also make for a very bad habit. Now they can be kept unaware of that aspect; again a slight, but meaningful, elimination of a century-old distraction.

So here's the twentieth-century actress: She knew when the camera was rolling, she knew how close the shot was, she struggled to be as natural and relaxed as she was in rehearsal, and she knew that film is money, so she wanted, *needed,* to get it right in as few takes as possible. And she needed to maintain her concentration while the crew had to stop and reload the camera. The camera rolled, the director called "Action!" and she was on: It was showtime. As Katharine Hepburn once observed, "I think you either can do it or you can't do it . . . I don't think it requires any special brilliance."

Now here's the twenty-first-century actress: She walks on the set, she's relaxed because she knows that there's no film in the camera, and maybe the camera's so small that she barely notices it's in the room. Then she "rehearses," knowing that anything that happens, any inspiration, any surprises, will be "on film." Maybe there's no rehearsal at all; maybe the director doesn't even say "Action!" Maybe there are no other crewmembers on the set; maybe she's even in a public place—a restaurant, say—because none of the "real people" around notice the camera. If she forgets a line, she doesn't apologize to the director or the other actors, she just goes on with the scene—the way we all do in real life. In fact, real life is all that interests her and the director, because there's virtually no difference between reality and performance: A visitor to the set would not know whether she's acting or not.

And neither will the audience.

baby (spot) A 500- to 1,000-watt **Fresnel** light.

baby plate This piece of equipment, known in New York City as a *pigeon,* has almost as many names as it has uses. Originally designed for mounting baby fixtures to the top of set walls, it is also used as the world's lowest stand by nailing it to a floor or on an **apple box.**

"back to one" The universal request to the actors and crew to go back to their positions (*see* **mark**) at the beginning of the scene. To be perfectly accurate, the phrase is used only for the actors; the camera crew would be asked to reset. But almost nobody splits that hair, so it's usually "Everybody back to one."

balloon tires Circles under an actor's eyes.

banana Here, an actor is requested to walk (or run, or stagger, whatever) along a curved path to or from the camera, *even if there is no apparent reason for doing so,* in order to avoid blocking whatever needs to be seen behind him, thus saving the camera department's bacon. The technique should not pose a problem for even the most Method-marinated performer. The request is normally something like, "Say, could you just banana left as you walk away?" or "Hey, do a banana for us there, will ya?" There's a right banana and a left banana but, of course, no "reverse banana." (*See also* **Groucho.**)

bar A horizontal metal tube from which lighting equipment or scenery is suspended. (Also called a *barrel*, *batten*, or *pipe*.) A batten is also a narrow strip of wood or metal that fastens or makes secure the lighting or scenery, as in "batten down the hatches" of a ship.

barn doors Movable flaps attached to lights to help shape the beam.

barney An insulated cloth cover for the camera, usually used in cold weather to keep it warm, and sometimes just to quiet it down a bit. A vestigial cousin to the *blimp,* the bulging housing formerly used to silence camera noise—and no longer necessary with most modern equipment. While the origin of "blimp" seems self-evident, barney appears to have been derived from the popular cartoon strip *Barney Google,* created in 1919. Barney Google, a sportsman involved in horse racing and boxing, had a horse named Spark Plug who was typically seen almost totally covered by his horse blanket.

Barney and Spark Plug

Barney   Spark Plug

base camp An area, as near as practical to the set, where the actors' trailers, food facility, **honeywagons,** main equipment trucks, and crew cars, etc., assemble.

Bay-o's Producer Jerry Bruckheimer–originated term for automatic-weapon fire, rumbling car engines, and military-sounding jargon, deriving from his director Michael Bay's trademark penchant for such things.

beef The power of a light. "Give me some more beef on the baby."

beefy baby A heavy-duty 2K stand without wheels.

below-the-line items Crewmembers or money budgeted for them, as well as for all other aspects of the technical side of production, preproduction, editing, postproduction, etc. (*See also* **above-the-line items.**)

best boy The second-in-command of an electrical or **grip** department, and the one stuck with the paperwork. This lieutenant of grips is also in charge of the equipment, hiring and firing the crew, and delegating tasks. Legend has it that the term derives from early days when crews were recruited from the docks and the request was something like, "Come on over to Paramount tomorrow and bring your best boy." The PC version, **best girl,** is rare and unlikely to enter the lexicon. (It's probably more sexist to call a woman "best girl" than "best boy"; let's just let it go at that.)

BFL Big Fucking Light. Any of the larger, heavier lights on a set. As in, "Let's wrap the BFLs early tonight." Sometimes bowdlerized as Big Fat Light. During the first seventy-five years or so of filmmaking, huge arc lamps (*see* **Klieg eyes**) were ubiquitously used. These were commonly referred to as brutes or goons.

B.G. Background, as in "Put 'em in the B.G." or "Get out of the B.G.!" Also used to describe the **extras,** but this can seem insensitive if they actually hear you. Calling these underpaid, hardworking, and long-suffering souls background, or even extras, to their face is demeaning, too: "Bring in the background!" or "Bring in the B.G." A more considerate term—heard too seldom—is *background artists*. Also referred to as *atmosphere*.

billy clip A vice-grip with flat plates attached, often used for holding a scrim or a **flag.** Named for its New York inventor, Billy Miller.

blackwrap Black aluminum foil used either to mold the direction of lights or as heat insulation. A late-twentieth-century invention, and here to stay. In New York, blackwrap is sometimes referred to as Run DMC (after the black rap group).

block Someone should write a book about this, but no one has; maybe no one could. Blocking a scene is, simply (one hopes) deciding where the actors should stand, move, and say their lines, where the other action should take place, and where the camera(s) should go to follow them. Ten different directors (and their actors and **D.P.s**) would block the same scene ten different ways.

Next to the choices made by the actors for their performances, this is probably the most arbitrary, personal, random, and inventive aspect of filmmaking. Some directors are storyboarders; others are totally freestyle, improvisational, and **on the day**—like me. No approach is right; only the result is.

block-shoot To shoot a scene or, more often, a series of scenes by filming everything that needs to be shot in one lighting direction before turning around and shooting in the other. This is a big time-saver, but isn't used much because it demands a very high degree of preparation and organization on the part of the director (and, one must hasten to add, the script supervisor). The most prodigious example of this that I've ever heard of was *12 Angry Men*, which essentially took place in one room. Director Sidney Lumet block-shot *the whole movie,* filming everything on one side of the room first, then turning around and filming the other side. Amazing.

blonde A 2K light, originally made by the Ianiro Lighting Company in Italy, and now any 2K open-faced light. Another term of unknown but evocative origin.

blow To overexpose the exterior of a window or doorway so as not to be able to recognize the background—the image goes milky-white. It is an accepted cinema convention, unrecognized by the general audience. Useful on sets when time, money, or conditions prevent seeing a realistic view. Especially useful in **poor man's process.**

blow job The act of cleaning a lens (or other piece of camera equipment) with a can of compressed air.

bobbinet Black mesh cloth used for darkening windows and for scrims.

bone me Crew slang for "screw me," or to get in one's way; almost always heard in the negative and in reference to the demands of one's job, as in "Don't bone me with that C-stand."

boom man Not always a man, this is the person who holds aloft the **fishpole** that positions the microphone that follows the actors wherever they go (unless they're body-miked with radio mics).

Height and armpower are required, hence the traditional male domination of this role. (But wait! *See also* **sound mixer.**)

boom up To raise the entire camera when it is mounted on a crane or dolly. (To lower the camera is to "boom down.") Not to be confused with a **tilt.**

bottle episode An episode of a television show where the cast never goes outside. *Cheers* is an obvious example of a show that employed this regularly.

box rental An allowance or extra payment allotted to a crewmember for furnishing special equipment or providing other materials for use on a film. The grip's special equipment or the makeup person's bag of tricks would be compensated as box rental.

B-roll The unprinted takes held on a separate roll of film. Sometimes forgotten, but sometimes returned to in desperation, when, like buried treasure found in the desert, some useful moment is discovered—unprinted but recorded—on the B-roll.

break film To stop filming for a moment to send the exposed film to the lab in time to process it for viewing the next day. The shooting day may be starting at any time of the day or night, but labs generally operate during night hours, so it's important to get as much of the film to the lab as possible by the time the developing and printing process begins. Thus, we "break film" at, say, five o'clock in order to drive, fly, or otherwise deliver it.

The derivation of the "break" is either conceptual (a pause in the shooting) or—more likely—literal (to break off the exposed film, still in the camera, leaving the rest usable as a **short end**).

break its neck The hanging of white silk sheets in front of lights to create diffusion.

breakaway Any item used in a stunt that can be safely and easily broken. Usually refers to glass, but it can be wood, metal, rope, plastic, etc. The name goes back to the earliest days of filmmaking when props were made of yucca wood, which, according to a 1928 production note, was "so light that it will do no harm when a comedian is clouted with it."

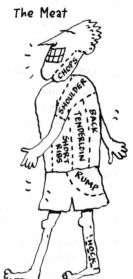

The Meat

breathing Rapid focus fluctuations caused by film fluttering in the camera gate.

bring in the meat An unnecessarily crude way of calling for the actors to come to the set. Certain to number the **A.D.**'s days if overheard by said actors and, therefore, rare.

broad A regular light, used for fill.

brodkin Used in New York beginning in the 1960s to describe a close-up even closer than a **choker.** Named after the late Herbert Brodkin, whose series *The Defenders* and *For the People* were stylistically distinguished by the use of extreme **close-ups.** (*See also* **double brodkin.**)

broom it Almost the same as **lose it,** but with a kinder, gentler connotation. Probably the most polite way of asking for something to be removed from the set.

bubble A light of any type.

budget The projected cost of a film, and usually a rule doomed to be broken. The charade here is that an initial budget reflects the realities of making the film. To be honest, it's a waste of time to "budget" a movie early on. When asked what a movie will cost, simply say, "Whatever you're willing to spend." A movie can be "made" for virtually any amount of money, and one will usually get what one pays for. You could make *Titanic* for a million dollars instead of a hundred-million-dollar version of that script; it just wouldn't be very good. (*See also* **good, fast, cheap rule.**)

The selling of a movie project is essentially an auction: The producer is looking, generally, for the best deal; the most amount of money. The financier is trying to make it for as little as possible. It's an absurd situation:

An executive, whose sole job is pretty much to evaluate what the cost/return of a movie will be, asks the seller (producer) what the product will cost. Underlying the discussion is, "What is it worth (to the studio) to have this movie?" A better "budget" is simply the amount of money available; that's what it eventually comes down to anyway. Then it's simply a decision whether to make the movie or not, given the results that the "budget" will yield. Unfortunately, the studios' and financiers' habit of asking what the budget will be is so entrenched in our cinema culture, it will take a lot to change it.

buff & puff To send an actor to hair and makeup. (*See also* **last looks.**)

build On movie sets, things aren't usually fabricated or made . . . they're built. Thus, the wardrobe department either shops for clothes and costumes or they "build" (i.e., create) them. A **set** is either a **practical** or a build. Want a special prop made, say a ray-gun or a jeweled crown? "That's a build."

bullshit glass The cameraman's contrast glass: a sort of monocle of very dark, smoked glass used to look directly at lights or the sun. Named for the lighting predictions made after looking through it.
   Historical Note: The great cinematographer Jack Cardiff writes in his book *Magic Hour:* "It's remarkable how early cameramen used to judge light level by eye alone but, even more remarkable, Billy Bitzer, the great

cameraman of silent films who worked with D. W. Griffith on classics like *Birth of a Nation,* used to take the exposed film home and develop it himself!"

bump A daily salary increase owed to a player—usually an extra or day player—for saying a line, performing a special skill, or some other extra contribution, such as wearing one's own special clothes, driving a car, etc. Bumps are seldom negotiated but are mandated by union agreement. Sometimes used when referring to crew positions, as when a camera assistant is bumped up to operator for a day when a second camera is needed. While technically possible, there is no such expression as "bumped down." (*See also* **adjustment.**)

butterfly A large piece of silk or net. Also known as a **windbag.**

butterfly lighting A high, diffuse lighting source centered on an actress's face to minimize skin flaws, nose shadows, etc., and (hopefully) accentuate cheekbones and beauty.

C47 Probably the oldest unmodified piece of filmmaking equipment still in use: a wooden clothespin. One legend has it that an accountant, tired (or afraid) of explaining the purchase of a large quantity of clothespins, called them C47s on the purchase order. Another story is that since they are often tossed from one crewmember to another (**flown,** in set parlance), they were named after the WWII military version of the DC-3.

Ubiquitous on sets, from the meanest to the most high-tech. There is a more modern version of the C47 called a *grip clip*. It's made of metal and probably more useful, but not nearly as cool.

An inverted clothespin is called a *C74*. Seriously.

car mounts Various attachments and devices used to position the camera(s), lights, and other equipment needed to shoot on a moving car. The time required to rig these—and to remove them—is almost always seriously underestimated. One of the persistent illusions presented to the director by enthusiastic **grips** and **D.P.s,**

this is often accompanied by the sinking realization that half a day's shooting time has been wasted.

Usually abbreviated as simply mounts: "Do you want mounts?" A handier alternative is the flatbed: a low-slung trailer towed behind a camera truck.

A special peeve of mine is the very natural tendency of actors who are "driving" a towed vehicle to move the steering wheel back and forth in a subconscious effort to simulate driving. Real drivers, especially when going straight down the road, barely move the wheel at all. Sometimes it's hard to deprogram this habit from certain actors, but it drives me crazy.

cardellini A clamp, made for grips and designed by San Francisco grip, Steve Cardellini. So ubiquitous on sets that it's called only by his name.

casting couch The piece of furniture in the producer's office where actresses were "auditioned."

Casting couch

While this was probably a very real item at one point, the concept is now more mythic than actual. But I'm not so sure about that.

Castle Rock Rule The theory, promulgated by the eponymous production company, that there are four kinds of movies: good ones that work, bad ones that work, good ones that don't work, and bad ones that don't work. (Work = make money.)

It's hard to make a good movie that works, but, then again, most good ones actually do work. Some filmmakers have the knack for making bad ones that work, but it's a special skill and seems to be one you're born with rather than learn. These filmmakers seldom use their power, money, or independence to join the group who make good films. No one who makes bad films that don't work lasts very long, and those who make good films that don't work are forgiven and often lionized even beyond their admirable attempts; so the best bet seems to be to make good films and hope that they will work, which they usually do.

This is a much preferable counter-rule to the old saw that "Nobody starts out to make a bad movie," usually invoked by those who actually did start out to make—and ended up with—a bad movie.

It has been argued that Castle Rock went out of the film-financing business by not following its own rule.

Central Casting Corporation, The Formed in 1926, this company still exists as a source of extras and bit players. It's located in Burbank, California, also the location of the studios of NBC, Universal, Disney, and Warner Bros.

Century lights Commonly used spotlights. The name is not derived from the fact that they've been used for a century—it refers to the original company, the Century Lighting Company, which no longer exists since being taken over by Strand Lighting. (*See also* **C-stand.**)

CGI **C**omputer **G**enerated **I**magery. The digital technique responsible for re-creating the *Titanic,* putting leg braces on the young Forrest Gump, and almost making you believe the Hulk.

charlie bar A length of wood dowel or thin plywood used to create a soft shadow, such as a mullion or branch. Also used to make a shadow cross an actor's face. These are also known, not surprisingly, as sticks.

cheat A quotidian practice on movie sets, capitalizing on the fact that the audience only sees what's on the screen, not where or when it was actually shot, or what's outside the frame. Thus, actors may be asked to cheat their look or position by looking or standing somewhere solely for the benefit of the camera (or the editor). This doesn't apply only to actors: You can cheat a lamp to the left, for example; you can even cheat a chair out of the frame entirely—even though it was supposed to be there.

Warning: This necessary device is to be approached with caution when dealing with serious Method actors or their ilk. Despite the fact that the concept here holds no moral value, it seems that while it is possible for all actors to imagine themselves or others as being werewolves, ghosts, or pedophiles, it is practically morally offensive to some Method actors to stand where they had not stood in the master shot, to imagine another actor being there (when he has, for example, gone home), or to look left when in the previous shot they had looked right. It might have simplified things if a less ethically charged term had evolved for this simple maneuver.

The Method actor's sometimes tenuous grasp of movie fakery is no doubt a self-protective reflex. The uncomfortable truth, of course, is that *the whole movie is a cheat.* It sometimes helps for the director to remind the actor of that fact, then discreetly wait a few minutes for it to sink in.

check the gate   To check inside the camera for any dirt, emulsion, or possible scratching of the film before printing the final take of a setup. The gate is real and metaphorical. It's the final order of business before moving on. (*See also* **hair in the gate.**)

cherry picker   A crane with a basket on the end—usually rented from a non-movie source. Not normally used as a camera platform, but rather for holding or rigging lights, elevating equipment, etc.

chicken coop A six-lamp lighting fixture, hung over a set for broad, downward illumination. A name derived, as you can guess, from the heating lamps used for chicken coops.

chinese dolly A dolly shot that moves laterally across the scene or action. This term was outlawed on the Universal lot a few years back for being politically incorrect. The rest of the industry has followed suit.

chippies On British sets, the crewmembers who lay dolly track.

choker A close-up that is framed from, or sometimes above, the upper neck. Sometimes referred to in scripts as an ECU, or extreme close-up, by misguided screenwriters trying to tell the director where to put the camera. This is mainly a literary conceit; on the set, calling for an ECU or even an "extreme close-up" would sound, to most ears, amateurish. Also referred to as a screamer.

Choker

Warner Bros. haircut   Choker   Cowboy   Cowboy Under restraining order

cinema Try to avoid using this word on any American movie set. (*See also* **mise-en-scène; movie.**)

circus In Canada and England, the same as **base camp.**

civilians Anyone not employed in the movie business. Not a pejorative term, just a somewhat patronizing recognition of their benighted outsider status. Not to be confused with **noncombatants.**

classic Hollywood cinema "A Jewish-owned business selling Roman Catholic theology to Protestant America." —Anonymous

clean A shot is either **clean** or **dirty,** depending on whether there is anything on camera (usually the other actor) in the foreground. A dirty single would be the same as an **over.**

clear the lens An admonition, usually to the crew, to get out of the way of what the camera operator is seeing or wants to see, usually while lining up a shot. This is one of those many expressions that only the cast and crew understand; an uninformed visitor would have no clue, but for the fact that the order is usually accompanied by a lot of arm waving, pointing, and shouting.

The opposite request, almost always issued in a civilized, polite, and calm manner—because it is only meant for the actors—is **find the camera** or **find the lens.** This simply means that, to put it plainly, "If you can see the camera, the camera can see you."

clearing the eyeline Actors on camera often have a hard time when they notice anything or anyone besides fellow actors. This is understandable, as concentration is often the most important, and difficult to achieve, of the actor's tools. Considerate (and very professional) crewmembers, when finding their job involves placing them near an actor's eyeline—or even close to the set— during an emotional or intimate scene, will face away or crouch out of sight during the scene.

Clearing the area behind the person or point in an actor's field of view is usually the **A.D.**'s responsibility and should be done as discreetly and as often as possible, not just when asked for, but as a matter of good manners. Not many actors ask for this courtesy, and it's often perceived as prima donna-ism—but only by those who have never tried to perform in front of cameras, lights, crew, and passersby. If you're working with an actor who is ultrasensitive to this problem, they'll let you know it.

Warning: Directors should take special care to clear themselves from their actors' eyelines; it's easy to forget, as the director's natural resting place is often right there. On the other hand, some performers—especially actresses, in my experience—are particularly eager to have the director in sight during a take. The film director is, after all, the only audience for the actor. One of the often-unspoken frustrations of good actors is to work for a director whose face is buried in the video monitor during the take. (*See also* **video village.**)

clock To rotate an object (a chair, a lamp, a prop); usually so that it's more convenient or photogenic. Seldom used when talking to actors.

closed set A **set** that is open only to the cast and crew. A more intimate version is a set that has been cleared of all but the most necessary crew—usually for a scene that includes nudity or extremely emotional content. Then it may be only the director and camera crew—or even fewer, if, for example, the director is operating the camera.

close-up The building block, garden-variety, one-size-fits-all of shots. D. W. Griffith is credited with inventing the close-up. (It's unlikely that he actually did; rather, he probably appropriated it and made it a part of the filmmaking vocabulary.) Griffith also brought the camera up close to the action, frequently cutting off the actor's feet at the bottom of the frame. This audacity was considered by many critics as an act of cinematic barbarity. In the same vein, some producers felt it a waste of money to hire an actor and not put all of him in the picture. Some films, and much of television, seem to be comprised mainly of close-ups. Collect as many as possible while shooting, but in the editing room, use with caution: it's easy to overdose.

cold opening At a premier or first screening of a film, it's customary for the director or producer to say a few words before the film and to introduce the actors, the crew, studio executives, etc. Sometimes this is not done

and the film just begins without any introduction:
a cold opening.

condor An extendable boom arm, capable of hoisting
lights 30 to 120 feet high. The term derives from the
company that originally made them, but now refers to
many high-lift devices, such as **cherry pickers.**

cone This geometric shape with a circular base and
curved sides that taper to an apex is a common type of
floodlight ("high-intensity light") in various sizes, such as
senior cone, junior cone, and baby cone.

"continuity is for sissies" This is one of those
ubiquitous, smart-ass aphorisms that sounds cute but
carries two very high risks: 1) You could be right, and 2)
The continuity person (**script supervisor**) may hear you.
It's true, to a certain extent, that you can get away
with mismatches, incorrect screen direction, hair and
makeup flaws, etc. But no one recommends it. Jean-Luc
Godard's classic film *Breathless* proved you could make
a terrific movie by totally disregarding the grammar of
screen direction. More recently, *Breaking the Waves* did
the same. And *Jaws* is a lesson in the ability of drama,
direction, editing, and performance to mask the most
egregious mismatches in the second half of the twentieth
century. Try watching it just for the quality of the wind,
color, and sea condition of the ocean from shot to shot:
You'll be amazed at what you never noticed. (*See also*
"If they're looking at that, we're in trouble.")

cook the opera Preparing the story for a moving picture production. Obsolete, but cute; should be returned to its rightful place.

cookie *See* **cucoloris.**

coproducer Identical to producer, but with just a tad of diminution understood. Like a copilot, a coproducer is often just as skilled, possibly more experienced, and often even more deserving of the credit. But sometimes, as in the rest of life, the producer just got there first.

"correct me if I'm wrong" A preamble favored by tactful **A.D.**s when they sense (or know) that the director is about to make a very big mistake. Directors should be especially on alert when confronted with this query, as well as anything like "Are you sure that . . .?" or "Did you really mean . . .?" Such expressions should have the same effect—and presage the same results—as the whistle of a very large bomb dropping.

coverage An option, subject to the director's whim, the time of day, the editor's hopes, and the pressure of others, to continue shooting the same scene from different angles and different lens sizes. (*See also* **GWTW** *and* **master.**)
    Note: It's always best to consider, and often important to ask, the actors who to shoot first in coverage. Some actors are best right out of the gate, while others take a while to warm up, thus benefiting from the extra off-camera

rehearsal. All things being equal, I've found that actresses prefer to be covered first. I'm not sure why.

It's considered very bad form, if not downright unprofessional, for actors not to stick around for their off-camera dialogue. Despite this affront, some big stars, impatient for whatever awaits them offstage, are often indulged in this, as in many another, breach of etiquette. On the other hand, it's not necessarily a mortal sin to ask an actor if he or she minds working alone in this way, especially when you need to spring the other actor due to **turnaround,** etc. Some actors actually prefer it.

cover set An alternate shooting location to be used in case of rain or other unforeseen unshootable circumstances. Try never to start the day without one.

cowboy A shot that is framed from the holstered-gun level. This is one of the most endearing and endangered terms of its species; a relic of the halcyon days of the Hollywood western. (Also, loose cowboy: below guns; tight cowboy: above guns.) To "make it a cowboy" can refer to a man or a woman.

Perhaps destined for obscurity in the twenty-first century, the cowboy is still relatively alive and well in Europe, where it is referred

Cowboy

to in French as the *plan americain* and in Italian as *piano americano*.

Another usage refers to the *cowboy hit* (usually called simply a cowboy). This is used in place of a **squib** when shooting (with a gun). To do a cowboy, the "victim" actor instantly clutches the affected part of his/her body, simulating (and obscuring) the intended bullet hit and eliminating the need for a special effect. This is the familiar version of wounding seen in little boys' reenactments of "cowboys and Indians," though it's unclear whether boys learned it from the movies or vice-versa. The technique is useful on low-budgets and/or time-limited sequences, but it usually looks pretty phony.

crab dolly A dolly that moves on four articulated rubber wheels, without rails (and only on smooth floor surfaces), thus enabling it to crab sideways or diagonally.

craft service The department made available to provide buffet-style snacks and drinks to the crew throughout the shooting day. Not to be confused with catering, provided by an outside company, which serves regular hot sit-down meals that occur every six hours or so. Craft service is a crew position and craft service people are represented by the union **IATSE.** In Canada and elsewhere, both the service and its crewmembers are called, charmingly, crafty.

The name derives from the crafts (electric, grip, camera, property, etc.) that it services.

crossing the lens There used to be few breaches of set etiquette considered as offensive (or as amateurish) as walking in front of the camera while the director, **D.P.,** or operator was lining up a shot. Whenever it was unavoidable, it was de rigueur for the crossing crewmember to announce "Crossing the lens," or simply "Crossing," and failure to do so was an offense tantamount to boarding a ship without permission or not saluting a general. In those days no one would *think* of crossing the lens without this simple exercise of good manners.

A variant school of thought has the expression as merely mock set etiquette: a pretentious and unnecessary, if not dated, affectation. According to this approach, if you're going to cross the lens, just do it— quickly—and don't announce it. D.P. and operator attitude will quickly determine which school will apply.

crossing the line *See* **split looks.**

C-stand A three-legged, lightweight collapsible stand with an adjustable arm for holding lights, flags, etc. Probably named for the Century Lighting Company, which first manufactured them, originally in brass and very heavy. Another alleged derivation comes from the claim that there are a hundred (i.e., "century") ways to use one. And, indeed, there are.

Note: Although it's a common practice, it is antithetical to the design and just plain bad form to use a C-stand in any other way than its vertical configuration. Rigging the arm horizontally or obliquely should be unnecessary and is potentially dangerous. One often sees this misuse compensated for by the use of a **sandbag** or two on the base of the stand, or in the case of perpetual offenders, a tennis ball skewered on the unused end of the arm—the subtle but sure sign of the amateur.

Some C-stands have a sliding leg at the bottom, known as a mountain leg or rocky mountain, which allows this leg to be raised so the stand can rest on an uneven surface. (*See also* **Gary Coleman.**)

cuban A light, used at night, with a flag in front of it.

cucoloris A cutter with random, irregular shaped holes in it, used to break up the light, usually on a wall. One of the more delightful words in the lexicon. (Bastardized, in recent years, on some benighted sets as a **cookie.**)

Now It Can Be Told: A few years ago the late, great cinematographer, George Folsey (*Animal Crackers, Adam's Rib*) related to producer Linda Stewart his thus-far undisputed claim as

Cucoloris

1.

2.

the inventor of this device. Shooting a film in Greece, he noticed the interesting way that a misplaced ladder cast its shadow on a wall, and asked the grips to make him something portable to help break up the light whenever he needed it. The device this fashioned was dubbed a *cucoloris*, which some believe derives from Greek, meaning "breaking of light."

"Cut!" Like "Action!" assumable by the **A.D.** with a nod or personal signal from the director, but *not recommended,* because *the director should be the only one to call "Cut!"*

It is the height of bad manners and arrogance, and can be downright subversive, for an actor to call "Cut" for any reason. I don't care if the set falls down or if an actor has forgotten their lines or peed their pants. The most interesting things that happen while shooting are often accidental, and, unless otherwise arranged, no one but the director should call "Cut."

Warning: It's easy to get so caught up in watching a scene that a director neglects to call "Cut." This need be only a little embarrassing, and will inevitably be interpreted by cast and crew as artistic intensity or the eccentricity of genius, or will at least redound to the putative brilliance of the performers. A politic A.D. will always save the day, or moment.

More appalling by far is the mistake of calling "Cut!" instead of "Action!" or the rarer reverse confusion. This lapsus lingua requires an instant decision to either a) fess up to the dumb mistake or b) invent a plausible excuse for it.

There actually is a common alternative to the use of "Cut" at the end of a scene. It is known as the *end-slate* or *tail-slate* or sometimes *tail-stick*. Instead of slating the take at the beginning, the camera is left running at the end of the take and then slated before cutting. This device is usually used when the film remaining in the camera is perilously close to the expected length of the scene, or when the director wants to shoot a scene without the fanfare and attention that slating and the call of "Action!" necessarily engenders. End-slating is often useful when working with nonactors or children, or when shooting surreptitiously. It can be a gentle icebreaker when working with actors under self-imposed pressure, before unusually intense or intimate scenes, or when it just doesn't seem right to be clapping the slate and yelling for action. It's also useful when shooting multiple cameras, especially for major stunts. Some directors make it a habit to always end-slate and never say "Cut." Tail-stick is often pluralized as tail-sticks.

cut A transition from one scene to another (visual cut) or one sound track to another (sound cut). A late cut is made (generally unintentionally) slightly after the indicated moment. A delayed cut is intentionally withheld to create suspense or other effects. A straight cut is a transition from one scene to the next without optical effects.

A **smash cut** is a cut that transitions from one extreme to another (quiet to noise; calm to action, etc.). This is the most overused term in modern screenwriting, employed by the amateurish and unskilled to impose a (false) sense of excitement to scripts that don't otherwise contain it. *Advice to writers:* Just don't ever use it.

cut in the camera To shoot only enough footage in each take or camera position to cut the scene as the director envisions it. The result is to give almost no options to a studio or producer wishing to recut the film.

William Wellman once said that after the editing of his lean, tough gangster movie *Public Enemy* (1931), the unused film fit on a reel no bigger than his hand. John Huston and Richard Brooks were also among the masters of this high-wire act. Modern TV directors sometimes give this a try, but it can come back to bite them. Big-time.

cutter A long, narrow flag also called a *finger* that cuts off light, generally placed on a stand in front of a light. Originally, editors were called cutters.

cyclorama A curved, seamless backdrop (painted curtain) to give the illusion of sky or space, common in film and television. Always referred to as a "cyc."

dailies The day's work, screened or viewed in the cold light of the following day. These days, it's most often viewed on tape, not on film in a screening room. The term implies a kind of quotidian drudgery, more a duty than a treat. Hence, the disuse of the more urgent and anticipatory former nomenclature, **rushes,** as befitted a time when seeing and making films promised unanticipated delights.

Note: In keeping with industry tradition and delusion, dailies are almost always deemed "terrific." That said, there is a commonly held cynicism that the better the dailies, the worse the film will be. The same inverse reasoning holds that what's funny in dailies is doomed to be unfunny when edited.

A corollary view is that the suffering and pain of shooting is all worth it if the film turns out to be a hit. I call this the "crucible school" of filmmaking: i.e., "Out of this crucible of misery, nastiness, and abusive behavior will come a great work of art." Of this approach is born the tolerance—and perhaps the impetus—for a multitude of directorial misbehaviors; the yelling, insulting, berating, and insensitivities found all too often at the top. I hold that not only is this not usually true but that it doesn't matter . . . even if it were the case. All movies are hard enough to make on the physical and mental level: The hours are long, the time and money pressures relentless, the production puzzles and challenges enormous. There are the ubiquitous unexpected vagaries of health, weather, and schedule. The greatest pleasure to be derived from the all-but-absolute power of directing is the ability to use it to control the style, pace, and tenor of the fiefdom of the set. In short, you can make everyone miserable or you can make everyone happy to be involved.

Your life goes by—the clock keeps ticking around at the same pace—whether you are enjoying yourself or not, whether you are "suffering" for your art or not. At the end of the day, there is absolutely no control whatever over whether the film will be a hit or even be a good one, so if you haven't had a good experience—a good *human* experience—making it, you've wasted more than the money and talent and effort that went into it: You've wasted your life. Otto Preminger and Henry Hathaway would probably disagree, as would quite a few others who have seen their rude and abusive behavior rewarded by some success. No matter; the clock, as those dead men could tell you now, still moves. (*See also* **Castle Rock Rule.**)

Some directors don't watch dailies. I'm one of 'em.

dance floor An area covered with (usually) plywood to enable the dolly to move smoothly in any direction.

day for night An old cameraman's trick, no longer employed as much as it should be: filming in the daytime a scene which occurs at night, done with filters and a judicious pattern of lighting. One might think that this would be rendered obsolete by today's fast film stocks and the digital revolution, but it's now easier than ever to accomplish. Not as old-fashioned or as phony as some purists think. Try it sometime—you might be glad you did.

Because it was invented by American cinematographers, it became known in France as *La Nuit Américaine.* Immortalized in François Truffaut's movie of the same name.

day out of days I love the way this sounds, don't you? Like something out of the Bible, or a Philip K. Dick title. But it's nothing more than a budgeting device; a chart depicting the total days that the actors will be needed for shooting. I don't know where the term came from; it doesn't make much sense. But we're all lucky that it wasn't called *chart of days* or *days actors work*.

dektoring The roving, jittery camera style made popular—too popular—by the television series *NYPD Blue* and too many others. Derived from the original, equally nervous, but mercifully shorter commercials directed by Leslie Dektor.

D.I. Digital Intermediate. The catch-all reference to a range of processes in which a digital visual source is manipulated. This requires the film to be scanned into digital files then color-graded or otherwise manipulated before being transferred back to film. The great cinematographer Roger Deakins introduced the process on *O Brother, Where Art Thou?*, turning green fields into parched ones.

dingle A branch placed in front of a light to create shadows. Also called a *brancholoris*.

director The best definition I've heard was from Orson Welles: "The person who presides over the accidents." Interestingly, the word itself, as it is used in movies, is distinctly American. In Europe, it was associated with banks, schools, and factories, but not with films.

Note: Unlike the problem with determining a producer's contribution to a film, it is generally quite simple to determine a director's role in the production. Notwithstanding the very rare occurrence of editing-room miracles: *If it's a terrific movie, it was well directed.* Some producers, actors, and crewmembers will quibble (at the least) with this axiom, but it's as close to dogma as you can get.

Every director works differently. For example, contrary to image and most practice, it is not even necessary for a director to watch a

Director and his A.D.s

scene being shot; nor is it unheard of for a director to just *listen* to the actors. A few directors have disported themselves this way as a matter of habit, some out of necessity (e.g., John Huston on *The Dead,* Christopher Reeve on *In the Gloaming*). Many more have found themselves doing it inadvertently out of fatigue, boredom, or a kind of directorial rapture wherein something other than the scene at hand is going on in their heads, such as the next scene or tomorrow's schedule, or the seventh hole at Bel Air. Taking this syndrome one giant step further, and embracing the nascent video revolution, Francis Ford Coppola—who once described his job as "running in front of a moving train"—directed an entire movie, *One from the Heart,* from video monitors inside *The Silverfish,* an Airstream trailer parked outside the sound stage. And Meryl Streep tells of having completed a particularly grueling take on *Sophie's Choice* only to find her director, Alan Pakula, asleep.

My favorite definition of the director's experience is François Truffaut's. He said that directing is a lot like he imagines taking a trip in the Old West on a stagecoach: You start out imagining all the exciting places you'll see and adventures you'll have—and you end up simply hoping you'll get there.

Such is the mystique, both real and imagined, of the director that—despite all evidence to the contrary, despite the fact that some directors are so inept and so insensitive that they should never be allowed to work again; despite the fact that a movie proves that the director is a total incompetent; even though the movie may be so bad as to be unreleasable—with very rare exceptions of death, decision, or despair, *no one ever directed only one film.*

This rule seems to have been broken almost exclusively by movie stars—John Wayne, Marlon Brando, James Caan, Charles Laughton—who probably discovered that money, power, and prestige are far more comfortably attained by remaining a movie star than by becoming a director.

On the other hand, there are many movie stars who have become excellent directors of multiple films: Laurence Olivier, Warren Beatty, Clint Eastwood, Sean Penn, Sylvester Stallone, et al.

Then there are Ida Lupino, Barbra Streisand, Jodie Foster, Anjelica Huston, and Diane Keaton. Notice something? There are only five of them and *there's no et al.* That's it: There are no other female movie stars who have become working directors. Yes, Sarah Polley, Penny Marshall, Lee Grant, Elaine May, Christine Lahti, and Julie Delpy have all made some very good films. But they are *actress/*directors, not stars. Just thought it was worth a mention.

director's chair The most useless and poorly designed piece of equipment on the set. Rickety, uncomfortable, barely portable, and unnecessarily tall; the deck chair equivalent of Short Man's Complex. Long overdue for a redesign.

director's cut The form of the edited film submitted by the director to the studio before outside (read: **star, studio, producer, preview audience**) opinions are accommodated or mandated. This may or may not be the same as the film you see at the multiplex. The director's cut is not to be confused with the **final cut,** which may or may not be the director's version of the film. (And which may or may not be an improvement on the director's cut.)

Incidentally, just because a DVD extra containing "extra" or "cut" scenes advertises itself as "the director's cut" doesn't mean that it really is. In fact, directors almost always drop scenes from the film in the editing process—and usually for a good reason.

dirty To include a part of an object—or person—in the foreground of a shot. The term may even have carried a metaphorical aura of moral judgment earlier in the century, when almost all close-ups, like the actors in them, were "clean." Much more in fashion these days. (*See also* **clean.**)

dirty old man A light-holder arm bent up.

Disney death

Disney death The temporary death of a character. The animation expression for bringing a character miraculously back to life à la Snow White or Baloo in *The Jungle Book.*

Disney squeeze Another recent addition to the lexicon: A process by which the **trailer** for a movie is optically "squeezed" from flat-format to **anamorphic** in order to be projected in the many theaters that are equipped with anamorphic lenses.

dog collar A short safety cable used to secure lights hung overhead. Called a *safety bond* in Europe.

Doris Day Parking The best parking space(s) on the lot. Though the phrase—like Ms. Day herself—is no longer in play, some things never change. The best spots on the lot are highly envied and highly protected. Never, *ever* park in a star's space. Both Clint Eastwood and Steve McQueen have responded with predictable results to the car, if not the driver.

A sign of changing times: It used to be customary to leave one's keys in the ignition when on the lot in case a car needed to be moved. Today, even behind security-drenched gates, everyone locks their cars.

I wonder if Doris Day had "Rock Hudson Parking."

do-si-do In **coverage,** to turn the camera around. Derived, of course, from the square-dancing term. Same as **roundy-roundy**.

double brodkin One more level of close-up intensity, basically from the tip of the nose to the eyebrows. (*See also* **brodkin.**)

D.P. The Director of Photography. Two schools apply: American and British. In the American school, the D.P. assumes control of all aspects of the cinematography, sets up the shot, directs the lighting, talks to the director about camera moves, etc. In the British system, the D.P. is a "lighting cameraman" (and called, actually, the D.O.P.) and the operator is responsible for setting the shots and the moves and communicating with the director. (David Watkin, the late, great British D.P., lit the whole set and then retired, often for a nap. The set, it was assumed, was ready to be shot from any angle. When he received the Academy Award for his work on *Out of Africa,* he thanked his operator.)

The term was invented in America when the DGA was formed and the then-members of the American Society of Cinematographers, not wanting to feel inferior, started calling themselves "directors of photography."

dress to camera To arrange or place an object (or occasionally a person) so as to see it best, within the shot, generally by moving it into the frame when it would not normally have been in view. (*See also* **clock.**)

dub In every country but the United States, it is understood that to dub a film is to replace production or, in some cases, unrecorded dialogue. In the U.S., however, the terms "dub" and "mix" have become interchangeable. Thus, the final dub and the final mix are identical. However, the temporary mix here is usually referred to as the temp dub. In postrelease context, referring to the language used, a film is either dubbed or subtitled.

Dutch A shot is said to be dutched when it is angled other than parallel to the earth's surface. It's almost always used for surreal effect—generally self-consciously, as when indicating drunkenness, psychological distress, or the victim's view of an attacker. But it can also make a hill seem steeper, or an airplane climb or dive (or a passenger in the cabin seem to be doing the same).

The name has nothing to do with the Netherlands. It derives from 1930s German cinema, where filmmakers used such severe camera tilts. They became known as *Deutsch* angles, meaning German angles, but the word was eventually simplified (and moved geographically) to Dutch.

Dutching is one of those directorial sleights-of-hand that should, like many magic tricks do, have a warning label attached: *Use at your own risk.* It also has no rules attached: tilt left, tilt right, ten degrees or forty-five; no one can tell you where to start or—more's the pity—where to stop. (The sole convention, only sometimes observed, is to tilt in the opposite direction when reversing camera direction in coverage.) Brilliantly used in *Citizen Kane*, overused ever since, Dutching is a favored ostentation of anarchists, car commercials, horror films, and MTV directors.

Duvetyne A heavy black cloth used for blacking out windows, hiding equipment, etc. Also called *commando cloth.* The main difference between the two materials, and it's not much, is the weight—commando cloth is heavier. (This is the kind of stuff that, frankly, you don't really need to know.)

"There ain't no answer. There ain't going to be any answer. There never has been any answer. That's the answer."
—GERTRUDE STEIN

Asking for Direction

LIKE EVERYONE, I grew up taking tests. Math tests, English tests, driving tests, entrance tests, and of course final exams. You name it. In my case, there were also various aviation exams: private plane, tailwheel, commercial, instrument, glider, seaplane, multiengine, etc. And for a long time I assumed that testing was the best way to know if you've actually learned something.

But some tests are given when you least expect them, for things that you didn't know you knew.

If I were the Provost of the University of Directorial Education and Licensing, I'd require that movie directors—like pilots, who must climb a ratings ladder—get their acting license *and* their producing license before they could get their directing license. But, of course, that's not the way the business works: Filmmaking doesn't have any requirements; anyone can do it. The only final exam is making the film.

Directors, meanwhile, come from many backgrounds and are often inexperienced in the acting or producing side of the art. Still, the most common prep school for quality directors is acting (Elia Kazan, Orson Welles, Sydney Pollack, Sidney Lumet); the next is probably writing (Francis Ford Coppola, Woody Allen, Oliver Stone, the Coens); then editing (Martin Scorsese, Robert Wise, David Lean, Hal Ashby). Very few start as producers. Curiously, almost no cinematographers have sustained distinguished directing careers—not for the lack of trying—despite the fact that theirs would seem the most likely background: working closely with directors, actors, schedules, and crew, and having responsibility for the telling of a visual story. Steven Spielberg, unsurprisingly, sprang full-blown from diapers to director, bypassing every stop along the usual road.

> Filmmaking doesn't have any requirements; anyone can do it. The only final exam is making the film.

The secret is no one is ready to direct. And even the most seasoned directors will admit that at times they dread going to work every day, knowing deep inside that they are about to be found out. That they're really a fraud, that *this time* it's going to be a disaster.

Even though they thought the exact same thing last time, too.

I was a charter member of the self-doubters club. And then, after decades of being tested, I finally discovered the secret of moviemaking.

It happened when I was directing a very difficult young actress. She would come to the set every day very prepared. She learned her lines, understood her "motivation," and knew every aspect of her character: what she would wear, how she would speak, how she would *act*. All well and good, I suppose, but when I asked her to try something a different way (after we'd rehearsed or shot it "her way") she would become intractable, argumentative, pouty, and, sometimes, openly combative. She just couldn't violate *her* image of the character; wouldn't even try a different approach or two.

After a few weeks on the set, the crew hated her, the producer hated her, and I truly hated her. Finally, after putting up with her whiny, preposterous behavior, I asked to see her after the wrap one day. I had no idea what I would say, other than to scold her, pull rank on her, and otherwise make her feel bad about the whole experience. I didn't really think it would help and I didn't care what happened. I was fully prepared for her to walk off the film or hole up in her trailer the next day. After all, she'd already complained to her agent that I didn't know what I was doing. Moments before our meeting, I wrote three words on a small piece of paper.

We sat down in my trailer and I handed her the paper. I explained the three words:

"The first word," I began, "is *Attitude*. Yours is simply the worst I've ever encountered.

"The second word is *Performance*. Your attitude is affecting your performance. It's limiting it to what you want to do, what you think is good. You're a good actress; that's why I hired you. My job as a director is to take you beyond that, to help you be great. And I've given up trying.

"The third word is *Career*. The combination of your attitude and your performance is going to affect your career."

She looked shocked. Frankly, I didn't care if she walked out right then, but she stayed, waiting for me to go on. I launched myself into the terra incognita of extemporaneous speech.

I started to recite the litany of complaints that the crew and I had. To my surprise, she didn't talk back, didn't argue, didn't cry. I rambled on. She sat and listened. I kept talking; she kept listening. Eventually I conjured up other films I had made, other directors, other actors, the many ways different people work. My pep talk was turning into a pretty dull lecture.

Then I ran out of things to say. Kind of embarrassing for a director.

Suddenly, the little train of thought in my head got switched onto a sidetrack and it dawned on me why she was having—and giving—such a hard time. Why she couldn't welcome the happy accidents on a set, the opportunities to change action or dialogue; why she couldn't allow herself the one unique luxury that film acting affords: to try it several or many ways and to go with the moment. I experienced the light of universal truth:

"I know what your problem is," I said, getting ready to share my epiphany.

She leaned forward, still silent, still attentive.

"*You think we're making a movie here.* We're not! We're just running film through a camera. Sure, we're *recording* your performance, but we're also filming all the hideous blunders, all the embarrassing screw-ups, all the amateurish flubs. But we're also filming the wonderful accidents—the ones that you couldn't imagine the night before when you were sitting in your hotel room learning your lines and working out your character and conjuring up your motivation. Then, when we're finished, we're going to take all that film—all those moments of inspiration and preparation and surprise; all the nuances and colors of everyone's performances; all the times you forgot your lines or tripped over the furniture—and we're going to take it back to a little editing room in Los Angeles and *then* we're going to make a movie!"

And that's just what we did.

And you know what? I think she's never been better than she was in our film.

ear To put a flag up on the side of a lighting unit. Also known as a *sider*.

Eastwood Rule An unofficial Directors Guild term. Shortly after acquiring his power as a movie star, Clint Eastwood tended to only hire directors who would defer to his wishes. He once famously banned director Philip Kaufman from the set of *The Outlaw Josey Wales*. Later, in 1984, he took away control of *Tightrope* from Richard Tuggle, whose name remained on the credits. The Directors Guild instated the so-called Eastwood Rule, which prohibited actors from firing directors and taking over themselves. The prohibition also applies to producers, studio executives, and anyone else associated with the production.

electrics The electricians. They are also called *juicers*, and known as *sparks* in England.

elephant door A large, sliding floor-to-ceiling door on the side of a soundstage, allowing the access of trucks, large equipment, sets, etc., or—one must forever imagine—elephants.

emily A **broad** or floodlight that has one lamp is called a single broad. The term was probably first used by a gaffer with an unmarried friend named Emily.

Emmy Television's version of an Oscar, presented via the voters of the Television Academy of Arts and Sciences. A feminized version of "immy": a nickname for image orthicon tubes used in early television cameras. The trophy was created by Louis McManus, a television engineer, who used his wife as a model.

executive producer Generally understood to be "the money," that is, the one who raises it, not the one who actually has it. On the other hand, this may be a title thrown like a bone to the production manager as an enticement. Often it's the star's manager, or the person(s) responsible for raising money or actually putting up some of it. Otherwise indistinguishable from **producer,** except in television. The credit of producer in feature films carries with it the qualification for Academy Award receipt. The Oscar for Best Picture goes only to the producer(s) of that film. In television, the **Emmy** is given to the executive producer(s).

extras See **B.G.**

eye A lens, as in "Take the eye out of the baby."

feature film A film of ninety minutes or more. There are dramatic features, animated features, and documentary features. Originally the term *feature* derived from vaudeville where it referred to the main attraction. The first feature films were a thousand or so feet long, and from two to eight reels in length. Ultimately, a feature was anything over an hour long.

fifty-fifty A shot in which two actors are seen facing each other in equal profile, at right angles to the camera. (So why don't they call it a "ninety-ninety"?) Sometimes the actors are asked to **cheat** their looks a little toward the camera, looking in the downstage eye of each other, which can cause problems. **Blocking** two actors so both performances are in the same shot is a challenge, but very often well worth it. *The Graduate* is

fifty-fifty

filled with fifty-fifties (and bold **one-ers** and **two-shots**), daring to eschew the traditional **over** whenever possible; it's worth watching for those two tricks alone. The fifty-fifty is often a big problem with actors who think they have one good side. Or worse, *only* one side.

Warning 1: Dueling good sides is a nasty game to referee; it might be wise to discreetly check with your actors before you start shooting.

Warning 2: Never ask Barbra Streisand to be on the left-hand side of a fifty-fifty.

fight your way in The (somewhat overstated but commonly employed) request by a **director** or **A.D.** for an actor or crewmember to get onto the set.

final cut A term used mainly as a legalism, referring to one party's contractual right to release a version of the film unaffected by another party's editorial requests. A handful of directors enjoy this power, as do an even smaller number of stars. Most of them abuse it. It's a pretty good bet that any movie a little over two hours long is the product of a director or star with final cut. At two and a half hours, that wager becomes a sure thing. No movie was ever too short.

find the camera *See* **clear the lens.**

fine cut A finished work or print, ready for final approval, prior to reproduction. An **answer print,** or first proof print, is between these two stages.

finger rule A cameraman's literal rule of thumb, er, finger, for determining how much sunlight is left in a shooting day. The technique involves extending the arm and holding the fingers together below the sun, parallel to the horizon. Estimate fifteen minutes per finger-width for each number of fingers the sun is above the horizon. Because fast-film emulsions can so easily accommodate light changes, or very little light, it's seldom used anymore. Too bad, as it bestows a valuable aura of Merlinism to the **D.P.**

first team The actors who will appear on camera in the scene to be filmed. Their **stand-ins** and doubles are, of course, the second team.

fishpole The boom man's pole, at the end of which is the mic (microphone). Sound departments have a panoply of terms referring to their equipment, especially the microphones: Sammy Davis, zeppelin, skunk, etc. On most sets, the **sound mixer** appears to be the key element of the sound team, the boom man just a kind of two-legged extension of the equipment. Most mixers seem to augment this apparent omnipotence with a demeanor and appearance that seems designed to maintain their insular sovereignty. The mixer sits huddled over his board (I've heard of female mixers, never seen one) encased in earphones (cans), fingers playing the levels and eyes glazed over in a Van Cliburn trance, the boom man and cable-puller slipping around the set, seeming to act only at his command. This is deceiving.

Historical Anomaly: Despite the paucity of boom women and the virtual absence of female mixers, the fishpole mic was invented by a woman: Dorothy Arzner, the first female member of the Directors Guild. In 1929, she directed *The Wild Party,* Paramount's first talkie, which starred Clara Bow. Early attempts at sound required the actors to station themselves awkwardly near mics hidden on the set. To permit Bow to move freely, Arzner had a microphone rigged to a fishing rod, effectively creating the first boom mic.

five-dollar Friday A ritual practiced on American movie sets; probably dating to the mid-twentieth century. At the end of the week, crew and cast members write their name on a five-dollar bill and put it in a hat, the winner to be drawn at the end of the day's shoot. It is considered snobbish for **stars,** producers, and directors not to participate; equally crass for them to collect if they win. Proper setiquette urges that they either match the pot, decline and draw again, or use their windfall to buy beer for the crew.

A variation of this is pool-betting on the week's big baseball, football, or basketball game.

flag An opaque cloth set in a metal frame used to prevent light from falling where it's not wanted. Also known as a *solid,* or a **gobo.**

flamethrower A cameraman who uses too much light. Rather rare these days. The tradition, however, is kept alive on TV sitcoms and reruns.

fleshing out the set The plasterer's task of filling in holes and cracks on the set prior to the painters doing their work.

flipping the lens Changing lenses. Derives from the days when the camera had a tripartite lens and all that was necessary to change lenses was to rotate it from one lens to another. Cool to say, and still heard occasionally, despite the anachronism. An even more colorful and poetic version is to "swing a lens."

float To place an object (**flag,** light, **gobo,** etc.) on the set by means of a lightstand or by suspending it from above. Implies a kind of movie magic, which it often, in fact, requires.

floodlight A high-intensity light, generally with a reflector, that fills (or floods) the area. Also a *flood.*

fluffer The charming, Disney-esque sobriquet for the person responsible for establishing and maintaining the necessary physiological condition of the male performer in

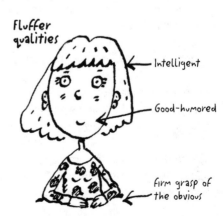

Fluffer qualities

← Intelligent

← Good-humored

firm grasp of the obvious

pornographic films. Seldom, if ever, seen—or even referred to—on nonporno films. But who knows what's going on behind the director's back? (*See also* **four-banger.**)

fly in To bring to the set or—if already there—to bring where needed. Most often used in response to a request: "Flying in, boss," if a person; "Flying it in right now," if an object. You don't hear it enough anymore, and it's a shame.

Foley Replacement sound effects such as footsteps, clothes rustling, doors closing, glass breaking, etc. Named after Jack Foley, the head of Universal Studios' sound effects department for many years. Contrary to popular belief, he did not invent the process. The job is performed by a Foley editor (a special effects specialist), who uses a Foley mixer to add to the action sounds like footsteps or collisions, recorded separately on Foley tracks. Foley work is done on a Foley stage where a Foley walker follows a performer and adds appropriate sound effects. Foley is also used as a verb to indicate the addition of sound to film, as in Foleying in. The credits for a Foley crew often appear at the end of movies, particularly in those with extensive sound effects.

foots Footlights along the front of a stage.

forties Grip trucks—with 40-foot trailers.

four-banger A trailer with four dressing rooms. Perhaps derived from the sound of doors slamming or toilet seats dropping. Alternatively, "banging" may derive from the alleged tradition of off-camera extras enjoying their "downtime." There are also two-, three-, five-, etc., bangers.

French flag A small black panel on an adjustable arm used on a camera to block flaring from lights.

French hours A form of shooting day during which no lunch break is designated. Instead, food is made available throughout the day (or night), and the cast and crew work continuously. Popular on low-budget and time-constrained films and, of course, French ones.

There is a downside to shooting French hours, however: there is no overtime. Generally, there is a limit of working twelve hours, after which the crew goes home. Occasionally, they may work an extra few minutes, or perhaps even an hour or so. But it requires special circumstances and a unanimous vote. Otherwise, they can—and will, if the concept is abused— just walk off.

French reverse A nifty trick, too seldom employed, of shooting a reverse against the same lighting setup as before. In other words, instead of turning the camera and actors around and shooting the opposite side of the set, you just rearrange the furniture, change the painting on the wall, whatever, and, voilà, you're ready to shoot the reverse: no time-consuming need to change any lights. Very useful outdoors, too, where the change in background can often hardly be noticed. Also known as a *Mexican reverse*.

On some sets you may hear this called a *Hollywood reverse*. Wrong.

Fresnels Commonly used reflected-light devices, named after French physicist, Augustin-Jean Fresnel (1788–1827). The proper pronunciation of his name is *Fray-nell,* though Americans say *Fruh-nell.* They produce wide, soft-edged beams.

full house When a light is too big or bright, causing lots of nets and scrims to be put in front of it. Alternatively, when a light has been dimmed down to its minimum.

futz In postproduction, a degrading of dialogue on the sound track via frequency limiting (**squeezed,** in mixer-talk) to give the quality attendant with voices on a telephone, radio, television, etc. Actually, the level of telephone communication and most TV speakers is so high these days that futzing is now just an artificial way of indicating, rather than simulating, that quality.

gack This word, meaning stuff, junk, trash, snuck across the border from Canada. "Get that gack out of the way."

gaffer Specifically, the head electrician. Generally, the head of any department. Can also be a verb, as in "Who's gaffing the show?" The term probably derives from early-nineteenth-century references to the long-handled gaff used by fishermen and dockworkers who were recruited by early studios, which used sunlight for illumination. (Southern California's perennial sunshine prompted the move from Chicago and New York.) The roofs of the stages were made of white canvas panels that slid open or closed on wires and rings. The "gaffer" used his long, hooked pole to operate them.

Some also believe that the word is derived from circus language, where the gaffer is the boss, or manager—which, in turn, may be short for *godfather*.

gaffer's tape In hardware stores across America, this silver tape is known as duct tape. But in Los Angeles—on set and in most stores—it's called *gaffer's tape*, and sometimes *grip tape*.

gag Any special rig or custom contrivance. Also, any unique form of action, such as a stunt. It has nothing to do with humor. A slap is a gag. An explosion that takes down a bridge is a gag. A car flipping end over end is a gag.

Gary Coleman A short C-stand; around 20 inches high. Named after the diminutive former child star. Gary has entered the elite movie speak society occupied by **Mickey Rooney, Jane Russell,** and **Jack Lord,** among few others.

gobo Any object used to hide or block a light. Technically a **flag** or a **cutter** is a gobo, but it can also be an object (vase, lampshade, etc.) rather than a piece of equipment. An actor can be used as a gobo, although many cameramen resist this as being too undependable. Gobo has always been one of my favorite words on the set; it was one of the first I ever heard. No one seems to know its origin, and it sounds so mysterious and special that I don't really want to know.

golden hour The time at the end of the day when the sun is low on the horizon: the loveliest time of the day for filming. It's often reported that *Days of Heaven,* Terry Malick's landmark film, was shot only at golden hour, but this is not the case: the **D.P.** was creative and resourceful. And, of course, it's not always an hour—sometimes it's less. Also called *magic hour*.

golden time Overtime: double pay. "We're into gold" is one of the production manager's scariest pronouncements.

"*Gone with the Wind* in the morning, *Dukes of Hazzard* after lunch" The **A.D.**'s gentle observation to the director or other crewmembers, usually mumbled in passing, that too much time was spent getting things done in the early part of the shooting day, and that the second half of the day will be spent desperately cutting corners. Generally an accurate, if predictable, assessment. (Abbreviated here as **GWTW.**)

"good morning" The universal greeting of the film crew, no matter the time of day or night, as long as it is the first encounter of the shooting day. If it is afternoon, you say "Good morning." If the call is for nine at night, you still say "Good morning"—but only when *first* greeting a fellow crewmember.

good, fast, cheap rule *"We can do it good, we can do it fast, and we can do it cheap. Any two, but not all three."* A truism, despite the glibness. Borrowed, no doubt, from another discipline (construction, perhaps), but always a useful promise to quote in the first budget meeting, the second half of the shooting day, and any other back-to-the-wall time.

Goofie

goofie A frightening, weird shot in a horror or mystery film.

go with the money To focus on, feature, or move the camera with the highest-paid (or possibly the most attractive) actor in the scene. Best uttered sotto voce from director or **D.P.** to camera operator, as stars don't need to hear it and the other actors don't *want* to hear it. A kissing cousin is the *money shot:* any extremely expensive shot or one deemed to be indispensable. Also, the climactic shot in porno films.

Greek To disguise an unwanted word (such as an obscenity or a brand name) appearing on camera so as to render it unreadable. An example would be to change the graffitied word FUCK to something like BUCK or BOOK. The request is to "Greek it." The name derives from the world of typography, where Greek or Latin "dummy type" is used to render text unreadable so the overall look of a typeface can be evaluated. Another alleged inspiration is that it refers to the expression "It's Greek to me."

Green Acres A disparaging description of the bright, front-lit, flat photographic style that so perfectly captured the quality of the characters on that TV series. As in (Producer to Cinematographer regarding an overlit scene) "This is looking pretty *Green Acres.*" Or (Cinematographer to Producer regarding an underlit scene) "Well, what do you want? *Green Acres?*"

griff Grifflon: a tough, rubbery material, stretched in a frame and used to reflect or soften sunlight. Usually comes in four sizes: 6' × 6', 8' × 8', 12' × 12', 20' x 20'.

grip A rigger, generally in charge of putting the camera anywhere the director wants it. The *key grip* is the person in charge of the grip department. Certain movie mythology credits the term to an early-twentieth-century film crew, recruited from the ranks of stagehands, who carried bags called "Grip and Go's." The name on the bag has also been reported to have read "Gripco," probably after a supplier. In any event, those workmen carried *grip bags,* from which the term almost certainly derives.

Grips are also the crew specialists assigned to the tasks of hammer-and-nail technology, the rigging of cameras and lights, and the moving of various equipment. The *dolly grip* moves the dolly.

gripology The art and science of gripping. More specifically, anything pertaining to the grip department. Need a wall moved? "That's gripology." Strictly set-slang, and not likely to be seen in print. (Except here, of course.) Additionally, the grip department itself is somewhat interchangeably referred to as *grippage.* Use sparingly.

Groucho To do a Groucho, it is helpful to have seen the mustachioed Marx brother's patented cigar-wiggling, crouching walk. Its on-set usefulness is in the service of the camera operator's reluctance to jerk the camera up in a close shot as an actor rises up from a sitting to a walking position or, worse, having the actor pop up out of a close-up to a crotch shot. Much more graceful for operator and actor alike is doing a Groucho, whereby the actor gets up and starts walking while still in a

Groucho

semistanding position. (The audience can't tell.) Even the most recalcitrant actors (*see also* **cheat**) are accommodating when asked to perform this little trick; probably because they prefer having their face continually on camera rather than a lower part of their anatomy. (It is also helpful, when necessary, to do a *reverse Groucho*.)

groveller A kneeling pad, usually used for the camera operator, when the camera has been placed close to the ground. In British Columbia, they're called *boat pads* because, well, that's usually what they are.

grumpy A light-holder arm bent down. (*See also* **dirty old man.**)

gullysucker A large, vacuum-equipped truck with a holding tank used for emptying the **honeywagon.** Not strictly a set-language term, but it's such a cool word it's good to know when the occasion arises.

gurney A cart for grips and electricians. (*See also* **taco cart.**)

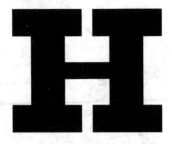

hair in the gate The discovery of a problem (but almost never, in fact, an actual hair; a piece of emulsion or some dirt is the usual offender) as a result of **checking the gate.** Usually announced with the same sense of lethal alarm as "FIRE IN THE HOLE!" or "BOGIES AT SIX O'CLOCK!" Virtually always cause for requesting an immediate **retake.**

handheld This would seem to be both a self-explanatory and an old term. In fact, the handheld camera is a relatively recent invention in the world of 35 mm features. The heavy, awkward Mitchell camera had been the industry standard for fifty years. Arriflex perfected cameras with reflex (through-the-lens) viewing systems, used first in Germany during WWII. American soldiers brought back captured cameras, and knockoffs began to be made. The original **Arri** factory in Munich, destroyed by bombs, was rebuilt, and production began again in the late 1940s. In 1972, Panavision introduced the 30-pound Panaflex and delivered the very first one to the set of

Steven Spielberg's *The Sugarland Express.* That same day, Vilmos Zsigmond, the cinematographer, took it off its tripod, threw it on his shoulder, and climbed into the backseat of a car.

Harold Lloyd set A set with only two sides: Why build it if you don't really need it? Named for one of the masters of silent screen comedy.

hero Never a person, always an object. Specifically, it's the actual object to be photographed or featured in the scene. The term is used a lot in commercials, from whence it probably derived. Often either a prop or something edible, saved to be photographed for its pristine qualities. It could also be the hero car, the hero hamburger, the hero gun—as long as it's the center of attention.

H.M.I. The norm in modern lighting, H.M.I.s are balanced for daylight. Almost no one can tell you what the acronym means, so here it is: **H**ydragyrum (that's Latin for mercury) **M**edium arc-length **I**odides. Drop *that* one on the electrical or camera department someday and see what happens.

"hold it" The most ambiguous of requests of the genre that also includes **broom it,** elbow it, **lose it,** and **kill it.** Implies only a temporary restraint, usually referring to a prop or other object. Directors should monitor the issuance of this request carefully, as some diligent crewmembers, once asked, tend to spend the rest of the shooting day—and sometimes the entire shoot—quietly "holding it."

Hollywood it To handhold a flag, cutter, reflector, etc., or to move something by hand, such as pulling a chair out of the path of the camera.

honeywagon The crew's portable toilet truck or trailer, coyly named, as if to spare a film crew's delicate sensibilities. The origin is from honey bucket, a slang term for a bucket or container that was used when a toilet wasn't available. (However, the restrooms on the studio lot go by the appellations "crapper," "shitter," and "can.")

Honeywagon

MEN WOMEN ANYONE WHO HAD THE BREAKFAST BURRITOS

Hoot A subtle, sustained turn of the head to the side while walking directly away from camera, thus identifying the actor (normally, a star). One might assume that this technique would be a Darwinian impulse for most actors, anxious to keep as much of their face as possible on camera at all times. (*See also* **fifty-fifty.**) Not so, apparently; it had to be invented. Named after the great cowboy star Hoot Gibson, for reasons now left in his dust. The director's proper request was "Give me a Hoot." The right or left version was usually left to the actor's discretion. "I don't give a hoot" is no relation.

Horace McMahon An undesirable, awkward
way of getting up out of a sitting position. The camera
operator's headache. Named after the character actor,
whose habit of bending forward then standing up made
the operator's job difficult. One might consider this the
opposite of the **Groucho.**

hose To cover a scene (after getting the **master**) in
roaming, long-lens close-ups. The request to "hose 'em
down" is a rather graphic, albeit accurate, request to
polish off the scene by grabbing as many close-ups as
possible with a roaming camera or two. Very useful under
time-limited constraints.

hostess tray A small platform for mounting the
camera on the side of a vehicle. One of an infinite array
of car mounts available to the director who needs extra
time to sit around waiting to shoot a scene in a car.
These mounts, their rigging, refinements, and removal
will take anywhere from two to three times as much
shooting time out of the day as you were told they would.
   Emergency Tactic: For the time-impaired director:
Rather than trying to watch (or direct) a scene in a car,
with the attendant vehicles, towing equipment, script
supervisor, video monitor, etc., just rehearse it thoroughly
with the actors, strap multiple cameras on the car, and
send them out on their own for a half dozen takes. If
possible, go along in the backseat and just listen to it.
You'll have plenty of footage to make it work.

IATSE The **I**nternational **A**lliance of **T**heatrical **S**tage **E**mployees, Moving Picture Technicians, Artists and Allied Crafts of the United States, Its Territories and Canada. Whew! No wonder they're so powerful: There's no one who isn't eligible to belong. This is the union to which almost all union crewmembers belong and must belong on all union films. Pronounced *"eye-at-see."* Chartered in 1893 as the National Alliance of Theatrical Stage Employees, it has grown like Topsy since then. The acronym has been mercifully shortened to **IA** for purposes of most discussions. The other powerful union in North America is NABET: The **N**ational **A**ssociation of **B**roadcast **E**mployees and **T**echnicians.

"If they're looking at that, we're in trouble." Heard all too often on the set, usually mumbled by crewmembers behind the script supervisor's back. Alternatively, it's a common directorial (defensive or dismissive) response to a script supervisor's observation that something doesn't match or is a visual anomaly. As director, you only need to say this a few times to diminish—at your peril—your crew's sense of professionalism.

indie While most people know that this means independent—i.e., not financed by the major studios—it's usually assumed that the concept of an independent production is more or less modern. Not so.

In 1909, P. P. Craft, an entrepreneur, imagined a spectacular screen road show. However, he soon discovered to his dismay that he was unable to acquire pictures of a sufficient quality to support the price of admissions to such a large venue. Craft then began to dream of making a film called *The Life of Buffalo Bill*. Negotiating a deal with the great William Cody himself, Craft set about to acquire the rights and make the film—just like producers do today. But after shooting copious amounts of film, it emerged that only Cody's outdoor Wild West show footage was usable. Undaunted, he assembled it in three reels and opened it in San Francisco. It was the first independent picture, and it was a sensation.

inky A small 100W or 200W Fresnel spotlight. Inky derives from "incandescent." Also known as an *inky dink*.

insert A close-up cutaway, usually establishing a story point, or meant to, such as the words on a page, bullets being put in a gun, etc. Sometimes used just to underscore a moment, like a hand on a doorknob. Often the filmmaking equivalent to a giant finger pointing at the screen, saying, *"Hey, look at this."* Some directors love inserts and use them well. Many more employ them as a lame cure for bad screenwriting or unimaginative camerawork.

in the can A reference to film that has been exposed (but not necessarily developed). Also refers to a movie that has completed shooting.

Question:

where's the film? where's the soup? where's the star?

Answer: in the can

Historical Note: Assumptions to the contrary notwithstanding, 35 mm film was first used in still cameras. In the mid-1880s, Thomas Edison had ordered his assistant, W.K.L. Dickson, to come up with a device to record and play back moving images to be sold as a companion to the record player. By 1889 he had come up with the Kinematograph camera, which used a hand-crank and sprockets to move film past the lens. But Dickson couldn't find a film stock robust enough to hold up under the stress of the sprocket drive. Then in 1889, George Eastman introduced the first snapshot camera to the marketplace. Dickson tried a roll of Eastman's film in his camera and announced to Edison that the problem was solved.

"it dies" Referring to the point, after which, "it dies"—where a shot or action is no longer useful or usable.

"it is what it is" A very common saying, acknowledging, often, "Well, I don't know how to make this (shot, action, scene, etc.) any better." Not as despairing or fatalistic as it might seem, it is also a healthy existential encouragement not to get complicated with a scene or a shot. "Don't overthink it" is usually good advice on the set.

Intermission

I GREW UP in San Diego, California. In 1940, when I was born, it was the beginning of World War II, and, for the next five years, I remember chickens in the backyard, margarine with a yellow dot in it that you had to knead, and soldiers and sailors coming to our house for Christmas and Thanksgiving. (My father would pick them up hitchhiking and bring them home.) And I remember airplanes flying overhead.

My sole extracurricular interests as a boy were sailing—particularly ocean-racing—and flying sailplanes. I had no real interest in the movies then; in fact, I don't remember going to many, except the ones my mother took me to: usually European films, especially anything with Alec Guinness in it. The Rio Theater was our neighborhood cinema. It was within bicycling distance of my house and it showed Saturday afternoon matinees of serials, like Hopalong Cassidy, Buck Rogers, and Roy Rogers; one after the other for several hours. Fifteen cents. For years, during the 1940s, I drew rocket ships and fantasized about space flight. I had no idea it would ever happen. The actual event, when the Russians accomplished it in 1957, was—and still is—the most mind-blowing event of my life.

I think the first movie I ever saw was *Bambi,* or maybe *Fantasia.* The first movie I saw that mattered, that spoke to me, was called *So Dear to My Heart.* But those serials, especially Buck Rogers and Roy Rogers, were exquisitely real to me. (Incidentally, we didn't have a television until I was eleven. No one else I knew had one, either.)

I didn't have any acting, directing, or writing idols when I was a kid, because I didn't go to many movies. In fact, I didn't really go to the movies until I was in them. But my earliest memory of an actor who I thought was really terrific is Montgomery Clift. I also, pretty early on, fell in love with the films of François Truffaut. And, although I've never had a favorite film of all time, I guess I'd have to put *The 400 Blows* toward the top of any list I'd end up making.

I dropped into Hollywood just after graduating from Notre Dame. It was 1962. I was an English and art major, but I had acted for fun in the evenings (there was no other fun to be had in South Bend, Indiana). Since all the good sailing jobs were taken when I got home, I drove the 125 nonfreeway miles north through the orange and lemon groves from San Diego to L.A. My grandmother lived in Hollywood, so it was easy.

I had a letter of introduction to a wonderful old director named Leo McCarey. Unfortunately he was semiretired, but his office was still on the Fox lot, which was deserted. It had been shut down in the wake of the way-over-budget ($40,000,000!) movie *Cleopatra*. Nevertheless, he was still showing up.

Mr. McCarey sent me over to the William Morris Agency where I was spotted by a young agent who took me to meet Bud Yorkin (the director) and Norman Lear (the writer/producer), who were casting *Come Blow Your Horn,* starring Frank Sinatra, looking for an actor to play his younger brother. The agent, Steve Yates, drove me over to the Paramount lot where I read for the part. They asked me to come back and read again and then again; then they gave me a screen test and I got the part. Just like that, just like I naively assumed it was supposed to happen.

In fact, that actually *is* the way it usually happens, but not after you've been in town only a few days, and not on your summer vacation. It was Bud and Norman's first movie, too—they had come out of variety television and would later go on to collaborate on *All in the Family*—and so we were all three, in exceedingly varied degrees, newbies. To this day, I still feel like the new kid in town. And I think that my penchant for working with first-time writers, producers, actors, and directors is my way of perpetuating that heady feeling of freshness and adventure that surrounded me when I first parachuted into that terra incognita.

Frank Sinatra was very, very generous to me. I was a completely unknown, untested, inexperienced actor, and he was arguably the biggest star in the world. He was an impatient man, but in my case he always had time to allow the director to give me an extra take. Sinatra was old enough to be my father although I was playing his brother, and he treated me like one. He talked to me like an equal, invited me to his home, and took time out to sit around and talk to me on the set. In fact, those being the waning days of the studio system and contract players, I was signed with Paramount and Sinatra's company for seven years. But after two years on my contract, I asked to be released, since it was clear to me—and to those who held my contract—that I had other things in mind than being a movie star.

It's not that I didn't work with great people back then. I had a good time working with Francis Coppola and Steven Spielberg in their early careers. It's always hard to tell whether somebody you know and believe in is going to become a huge success, but somehow I guess I knew because I had great faith in them. I acted for free in Steven Spielberg's first film—a little unfinished movie called *Slipstream* that he did before

Amblin', which put him on the map—just to help get him started. And with Francis, we were best friends before I acted in his first Hollywood film, *You're a Big Boy Now,* and I am still nuts about him. I acted for Terry Malick in his first short film when he was an AFI student, then hired him to write his first screenplay for the first movie I produced, *Deadhead Miles.* I still enjoy friendships with all those guys. And Bud and Norman—to whom I owe my career—are still my surrogate godfathers.

People are always asking me about movie stars, assuming I hobnob with them. I don't; never have, really. And I've tended not to work with them much as a producer or director. But while I was acting for a living, I worked with quite a few stars—stars of their day, that is, not exactly the kind we have today. Steve McQueen was one of the biggest stars in the world when I worked with him. Like Sinatra, he was very impatient, but we became friends. We had a common interest in old airplanes and classic cars; I later sold him a '34 Packard and a '36 Caddy that I owned. Jackie Gleason was a total professional and always an honor for me to be around because I knew him from television. I was not a fan of "older" movie stars at that point but I knew a lot about him. Dean Martin was everything that Dean Martin seems to be in his films and television appearances: fun, casual, relaxed, and always funny. Anthony Quinn was a very intense actor, but always treated me very, very well. I had a good time with him. Rock Hudson was one of the kindest, nicest people I've ever met, actor or not. He was a very big star at the time of *Ice Station Zebra*, but sitting around the set, he was just one of the guys among the cast of an ensemble picture. Warren Beatty, a star by any measure, is one of the brightest and most interesting people I've ever worked with. I ran into him a while ago outside a Venice, California, café, waiting for his wife to come out of yoga class. We sat and talked about our lives as if we were old college roommates: two older guys with beautiful wives and little kids.

Sinatra wasn't the first movie star I ever met; he was just the first one I recognized. I met my first one six years earlier, when I was sixteen and a scrawny kid hanging around the docks of the San Diego Yacht Club, the only place on earth I felt like I belonged, among the sailboats. And one afternoon, into the bay and up to the main dock, came one of the most beautiful boats I'd ever seen. It was a wooden (they all were then) yawl, about 55 feet long, beautiful lines, perfectly maintained, smoothly handled by the two men aboard. As they pulled up, I quickly scrambled over to catch their docklines and secure them to the cleats.

Then I just stepped back and stared at the boat, drooling, I suppose. One of the guys—the skinny one at the wheel—figured me out right away and said, "Hey, kid, you wanna take a look aboard?—take a look below?"

I must have mumbled something (I was incredibly shy then, and for many years, until Norman Lear commanded me to stand up straight and look him and others in the eye), because the next thing I remember was that the other guy—Butch or something manly like that—was showing me around the boat. While the skinny man poured himself a drink and relaxed in the cockpit, Butch gave me a tour. He could see I knew my way around a boat, could tell I was a kindred soul, and he treated me like the old salt that I wished I really were. After a few minutes I thanked them, stepped back onto the dock, and went on home. The next afternoon, when I went back after school, the boat was gone. A few weeks later I heard that the skinny guy who had invited me on board his boat had died. It was Humphrey Bogart, and that visit had been his last cruise aboard his beloved *Santana*. Then I kinda knew who he was, but to me he wasn't a movie star.

Years later, I owned a boat—a wooden yawl—that was only slightly more beautiful than the *Santana*.

Meanwhile, I made the move into producing because I just wasn't cut out to be a movie star. It is, in my view, more of a curse than a pleasure to be lionized at every turn, recognized wherever you go, praised by everyone and critiqued by none, given preferential treatment and indulged by virtually everyone, deserving of it or not. It wasn't the kind of life I would look forward to having and also I didn't enjoy waiting for the phone to ring for people to hire me. I was much less patient than that and would much prefer to instigate the making of any films that I was going to be involved with. I'd rather give the party than wait to be invited to it.

Considerably later than my peers, I began directing. And that's almost all I've done for the last thirty years, with only an occasional excursion back into the worlds of producing and acting. People are always asking me which job I prefer—as if I'd really rather not be doing what I'm doing, or as if directors secretly yearn to be producers or actors. The decision to produce a script is much like deciding to go out on a blind date. The decision to direct it is like deciding to get married.

> The decision to produce a script is much like deciding to go out on a blind date. The decision to direct it is like deciding to get married.

Deadhead Miles, Steelyard Blues, Hearts of the West, Going in Style: Those producer credits are personal to me. As was *My Bodyguard* and other movies, like *Untamed Heart* and *Five Corners,* both of which I directed. The production experience of *The Sting,* despite its enormous success and Academy Awards, does not hold a particularly warm place in my heart. It was a real "Hollywood" film: big stars, famous director, shot on the Universal lot; a relatively impersonal, chilly experience. I'd basically grown up on the Paramount lot, where I knew the guards, the department heads, the waiters in the commissary, and they knew me. Universal, with its black-suited executives and factory approach, was not my idea of a place to make a film. After our movie's enormous success, the studio held a party for everyone on the lot. I wanted to bring my kids, but there was a one-guest limit. I didn't go and didn't set foot on the lot again for decades. And *Taxi Driver* was really my partner, Michael Phillips', baby: once we optioned the script and set it up at Columbia (and waited two years for them to finally acquiesce to make it—for $1.8 million), Michael was the point man. That one turned out okay, too.

There is no strategy for making movies. You do the best with what you've got. Sometimes a movie that's close to your heart gets made and sometimes a movie you never imagined being involved with gets made, and they don't all turn out one way or the other regardless of how or where they are born—very much like children. I've never plotted a course in filmmaking, but as things have turned out, I have pretty much ended up doing one for me and one for them and one for me and one for them. But for me the making-of is vastly more important than the result-of. They're never predictable, and I don't know that any movie was tougher than another one to make. Looking back, they seem easy now. But they seemed impossible then.

I consciously seek out new talent. In addition to Terry Malick, David Ward, John Shanley, and Marty Brest, I've worked with many other people who were untested or new. The easy answer as to why I seek out young talent is that I'd rather go to a horse race and bet on the long shot than on the supposed sure thing. What's the thrill in knowing what everyone else knows? What's the pleasure in a foregone conclusion?

I loved the script of *My Bodyguard* because it had none of the cornball clichés of so called "youth movies" of the time. It didn't have any beach parties, surfboards, silly kids, food fights, fart jokes, or stupid adults in it. It was, I daresay, one of the first American movies about young people that was real and true; the first script by its author, Alan Ormsby. And it was a wonderful experience because it was a discovery of young actors who are today pretty famous. High school kids who had never acted before, like Joan Cusack, Adam Baldwin, and Jennifer

Beals. People who had acted only once in a film, like Chris Makepeace and Matt Dillon, and many other people who had never done it before. And I got to work with my dear friend Don Devlin, who produced it for me.

But there was a very dark side: The movie was, above all, a test—a personal test of whether, after all the movies I had acted in and produced, I had learned anything at all. I was pretty sure I had, but I needed to know. A few nights before shooting, I faced a huge moral dilemma: Should I admit to my producers and financiers that I was a fraud, that I didn't believe in the script or in myself, that we had all made a terrible mistake, that we should stop right now and cut our losses? Or should I pretend that I was a director who believed in the project and knew what I was doing? I silently agonized over this for the next forty-eight hours. Then I took the coward's way out, faked enthusiasm and conviction, and continued. The movie was a critical and financial success.

After seven or so years as an actor, working with many directors of note—Coppola, Spielberg, Hal Ashby, Sydney Pollack, Sir Carol Reed, John Sturges—I always wondered if I had learned anything from any of them. All I know is something must have rubbed off, because I'm still doing it. But I wish I knew what it was. Like everyone else, I imagine that there is a how-to book that every other director but me has read—or written. Everyone, it feels, knows more than I do, has more talent or experience, or both; and everyone else knows "the secrets."

I have no idea what my style or "theme" is. I think that the one thing I might call my theme is that it feels to me as if I've made the same movie over and over again. That movie is my first one, *My Bodyguard*, and the common theme is that I think I've always made movies about people who need other people—or think they do—to take care of something for them, as well as the need we all have to take care of other people. Big hits like *The Sting* and *Taxi Driver* are nice, but I'm always, always extremely pleased and not a little bit amazed that movies like *Five Corners*, *Untamed Heart*, and *My Bodyguard* have intensely devoted fans. People think that you get tired of hearing that they love one of your little, modest movies, but you never do. At least I never do. It's the next best thing to huge success. And maybe in the long run, better.

None of my films have come close to my original vision because I don't storyboard, I don't rehearse, I don't really know what's going to happen "on the day," so I tend not to have the kind of prescient vision that people attribute to the legendary directors. Rather, every film is a journey of discovery: what the movie's about, what the people are about, what the scenes are about. And I'm always surprised that they turn out well at all, much less as well as some of them have. None of them have been what I thought they would be, but in my book, that's a good and inevitable thing.

Movies for cable and commercial television have also been extremely rewarding—movies like *Oliver Twist* and *Whitewash* and *Beyond the Call*. I do wish I could have done each of those as a feature film, but they weren't intended to be features. I came on to make the best of them as the director, and I think I did. I'm not sure if they suffered from being on a very short leash, because, in many ways, constraints almost always make things better. In fact, I'm of the school that believes that constraints of time, budget, weather, etc.—all the things we agonize over and complain about—make for better films than the surfeit of money and time that most big-budget films, stars, and directors acquire or insist upon.

Another question I get asked is whom I'd like to work with and what my dream project is. The deal I might make with the Devil would be that if I could be allowed to work over and over again with the people I've already worked with, I'd agree never to work with a new person. But then, of course, think of all the chances I'd miss to discover new talent. So forget it. My dream cast is a bunch of great actors that nobody's ever seen before.

Jack Lord A 50 mm lens, as in five-oh, named for the star of *Hawaii Five-O*. (*See also* **McGarrett.**)

Jane Russell This should be self-explanatory, but probably isn't anymore. A shot framed across the middle of the chest, named for actress Jane Russell, who was known for her estimable bustline. (Howard Hughes personally designed a particularly levitating brassiere for her.) Colorful, but only if used sparingly. Downright phony if used by anyone under forty. The embodiment of **two Ts.**

jib arm A small counterweighted arm, usually mounted on a dolly, on which the camera can be secured and "floated" about in a small area.

Jonesy deck A flexible rostrum that was developed or made at Elstree Studios in the 1970s. It can be used as a camera platform, a walkway, and plenty of other utilities that require height and stability. As to who Jonesy was: It's one of the great unsolved mysteries of film history.

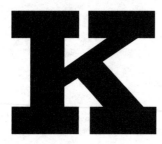

key The head of a department (electric, wardrobe, makeup, etc.). These are the people who need to be present at the production meeting and **technical scout.** (The key **grip,** oddly, is the only one who is credited as a key. The key electrician is the **gaffer;** the key camera person is the **D.P.** Go figure.)

The word can also refer to the key light: the primary, brightest light used to illuminate a face or set. Outdoors, the sun is often the key light. Its kissing cousins are back light and fill light.

kicker Usually a hard light used to emphasize obvious highlights, such as cheekbones. In England they call it, much more colorfully, a *basher.*

kill it Turn it off; cancel it. Usually in reference to a light, as in "kill the baby."

kiss Just a gentle touch of a light or a camera's frame on an actor.

Klieg eyes Soreness of the eye caused by the glare of studio lights. Arcane, but charming. Named after their late-nineteenth-century inventors, the Kliegl brothers, Klieg lights were high-intensity carbon arc lamps used for decades on film sets, making night appear to be day, and making every day sufficiently bright. Sometimes the powerful searchlights used for film premieres are still referred to as Kliegs. According to the book *Inventive Genius,* "Actors forced to work under the bright lamps created a Hollywood trademark as famous as the Kliegl brothers' invention: the perpetual wearing of sunglasses."

Inventors of the Klieg light

John H. Kliegl   Anton Kliegl

knock it down To take the shine or newness off something; usually immediately and temporarily, by spraying it with a dulling spray, often a hair product called Streaks 'n Tips. Then the request to "knock it down" is often simply reduced to the order "Streaks 'n Tips."

L

lab A catch-all phrase for any facility where film is processed. Motion picture processing plants were "factories" until 1907, when Jeremiah J. Kennedy, a consulting engineer and financial expert, went to salvage the unhappy Biograph concern in Hoboken, New Jersey, and raised its darkroom establishment to the status of a **laboratory.** "Because," opined Kennedy, "we can get a better class of people to work in a laboratory."

lamp down To replace a lamp with one of lower wattage.

Last Looks Tools

last looks
Final touch-ups to the actors by the makeup, hair, and wardrobe departments. Also signals the effects and prop departments to be ready to go. In effect, the **A.D.**'s notification to the set of the final moments before rolling film. Sometimes abbreviated as *finals*.

The *après*-lunch version, before shooting resumes, is called *touch-ups*, an operation that the makeup and hair departments approach with a time-consuming thoroughness that assumes the actors have eaten lunch with their faces buried in their plates while sitting in front of a blow-dryer.

Desperate Directors' Ploy: Want to have a whole extra hour—or more—for free in your shooting day? Just tell those three departments, and your actors, that they must eliminate last looks. The actors must be (the horror! the horror!) responsible for their own appearance between takes and/or those departments must check them out well before shooting is ready. You'll save at least six minutes an hour, and over a ten-hour day, there's your extra hour. You can get away with this on low-budget films, where you'll need that time the most. Don't bother asking most movie stars.

"leave enough room to get the scissors in"

A request to actors to pause at some point in the dialogue or action, just enough to make a cut in the scene that will look natural when it is cut away from then resumed. A good example would be an offstage glance, held a bit longer than normal. As with some other terms, it can seem an anomalous expression in this digital age. (Doubly so, as scissors were never used to edit.)

leaveright Shorthand for "Leave 'er right there"— as in "That's a leaveright."

Lewinskys Kneepads used by stuntmen. A recent addition to the argot.

"Lights, Camera, Action!" This expression is never actually spoken on a set—nor is it likely ever to have been. The expression may have its fictional roots in a long-ago era when arc lamps required a bit of time to warm up. Even then, there would have been a minute or so between the first two requests.

location scout A crewmember responsible for finding appropriate locations for shooting. Not to be confused with the location manager (who is usually not on set but manages the details of filming on location, such as power, parking, and permits).

Note to Directors: It is expected that the director will sit in the front of the van or car whenever the crew is transported. This is such a time-honored tradition that it would be considered reverse snobbism for you to sit anyplace else. (If it's a bus, you can break this rule.)

(*See also* **recce.**)

lock-off A way to really embarrass yourself on a set is to make a move anywhere near a camera that has been locked off—that is, secured to its mount in order to film an effect, such as a time-lapse sequence. The slightest jiggle or vibration can ruin the shot. I can't think of a much worse way to bring the attention and mockery—if not wrath—of the entire crew upon oneself.

loop Postproduction dialogue replacement using identical-length loops of picture, guide track, and recording track. The line to be replaced would thus repeat over and over, and the actor would go for a take when they were ready. Although the film technique is no longer used—everyone does it digitally now—dialogue replacement is often still referred to as looping. (*See also* **A.D.R.**)

A lot of actors have trouble with looping their lines; they throw up their hands as if being asked to recycle the plastic with the paper. Others have no trouble at all. It has nothing to do with experience or talent: Brando, for example, was a terrible looper. Some actors *hate* looping their lines, feeling it destroys the immediacy of their original performance; others look forward to having the chance to change or improve their performance. Many movies, famously, Italian ones, are customarily *entirely* looped. (Federico Fellini often talked to his actors over a bullhorn while they were performing, or played music to set the mood of the scene.) Usually a "loop group" of actors skilled in improvisational vocal work is hired in postproduction to simulate crowds and fill in the gaps for missing dialogue.

It's easy to use the word **dubbed** in place of looped. Try not to make this mistake.

lose it Almost the same as "kill it," but a tad less permanent.

Note: Equivocal requests on a set are often advisable. If you ask to lose a prop or a light, for example, you can bet it will not be far away when you ask for it again—and it will undoubtedly be asked for again. Often in the same breath. The director who asks for anything (or anyone) to be permanently removed from the set, or states that something will never be needed, is bound to eat those words.

Louma crane A lightweight, portable crane with a remotely operated camera head. A prototype was developed by Jean-Marie Lava**lou**, Alain **Ma**sseron, and David Samuelson in 1970, and it was first used in Hollywood by Steven Spielberg in 1979 on his film *1941*.

love Electricity. Plugged in. Rather than ask for the electricity to be turned on or plugged into a light or other device, some crews request "Gimme some love." (*See also* **beef.**)

lunch The meal served halfway through the shooting day. It doesn't matter whether the "day" began at noon and lunch is at 6 P.M., or whether it is being served at 4 A.M. or midnight. *It is still lunch.* Similarly, the shooting day is always called the day—even if it is actually night.

Lunch Protocol

BISTRO

Producer   Writer   Driver of the honeywagon   Background artists   Crew   Smart (but hungry) director

(*See also* **good morning; on the day.**) As with the **wrap** and the **Abby,** calling lunch is the **A.D.**'s bailiwick—one of his or her few undisputed pleasures.

Unwritten Rule: It is understood that the crew will line up for lunch ahead of the background artists, the cast ahead of the crew, and the stars ahead of the rest of the cast—or, more often, they will send someone to fetch lunch to their trailer. It is also understood that the director may, as at any other time, exercise his droit du seigneur and go straight to the head of the line. This version of "cutsies" is tempting, but the director's taking a place in line with or behind the crew will have a far more lasting effect on their working relationship than the few minutes otherwise saved.

Breakfast is normally made available out of a catering truck or at a table at the start of the shooting day—again, regardless of the actual time of day. The usual order is a burrito or a fried-egg sandwich. (Legend has it that this latter item was invented by a hurried John Ford on a distant location in the West.) The menu is generally limited to all but the director, who, once introduced to the otherwise oblivious servers, may request anything available—and then some. On low-budget films, and

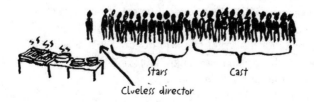

Stars

Cast

Clueless director

sometimes on the studio lot, the food truck may well be a commercial "roach coach," and the cast, crew, and director will have to pay for their meals.

If there is to be no breakfast (usually on a distant or confined location), the crew or cast is requested to report to the set "having had," a term that, like many set expressions, need no modifiers to be understood.

Even the lowest-budgeted film will still have a **craft service** table with doughnuts, cold cuts, finger food, soft drinks, etc. Failure to supply this minimal amenity is sufficient cause for crew mutiny. Failure to supply a craft service table that looks like the display case at Dean & DeLuca is considered bad form on any big-budgeted film and most commercials.

There is no such thing as dinner, only something (often pizza or other fast food) called a "second meal." This innovative and deceptively beneficent term was probably designed to give the crew a diminished sense of time passing. It doesn't.

Note: Distinct body language can be read during lunch. If the director, **D.P.**, and **A.D.** are seated together, a problem is likely to be announced soon. A visit from a studio executive during lunch is not necessarily a sign of trouble—but before or after lunch it may be seen as a red flag. Female stars often eat with their assistants, stunt doubles, or costars. The writer, if on set (a rare inclusion), will normally settle for a welcome at any table. It is unseemly for the writer to cut in front of the line with the director, stars, etc., before ingratiating himself with the crew, but no one will complain.

magic finger In England: a small wedge of wood used to hold open doors and level furniture on the set. Usually carried by the stagehands, standby carpenters, etc., its use is more precise than **Paganinis.**

make a meal of it Really get into it, or even overdo it. You can say this to an actor, but probably shouldn't very often. Sometimes heard in reference to the camera operator's chances to get complex with a move.

make it go As the expression implies, make it go away; a harsher variant of **broom it.** The opposite request, to bring something in or place it on the set, is "make it live."

Note: "86 it" is sometimes heard, but this lingo is out of place on a film set and should be relegated to the bars and restaurants that spawned it.

make the day To successfully cover all the scenes scheduled for the day, it's akin to "dodge a bullet."

In features, this always sounds like you've won the big game. In TV, it's expected. In either case, it feels very good for any director to hear this—but only in the past tense at the end of the day.

manmaker Any device (**pancake,** quarter-apple, etc.) used to make an actor taller. May also be used in reference to any crewmember (operator, grip, etc.) needing to be made a few inches taller for the job at hand.

Warning: While references to crewmembers' need of such aids are generally announced in the most blatant manner possible, references to usage with any actor is best whispered. Performers should *never* hear this word uttered.

Manmaker

thanks mom

mark When a scene has been **blocked** and rehearsed, it's time to mark it: to put down bits of tape or chalkmarks identifying the actors' positions throughout the scene, as well as the camera positions. It's good basic setiquette to remove these marks before moving to another **location** or **set.** Actors who don't hit their marks drive a camera crew crazy; camera crews who insist on actors hitting their marks drive actors crazy.

martini The term for the last shot of the day, the origin of which might seem self-evident—but it's not.

The martini actually refers to the saying that "The next shot is in a glass." Get it? The **Abby** cautions apply here as well, although it's pretty damned hard to get this one wrong if you've done a proper job calling the Abby.

master The entire scene shot from beginning to end, including all the actors, or as many as possible. This assumes an ability on the actors' part to remember their lines and their blocking well enough to get through the whole scene. (I once acted in a film with Steve McQueen, whose first question to the director—not at all rhetorical— was, "You're not going to do any masters, are you?")

With some actors on all days, or with all actors on some days, shooting a complete master may be close to impossible. A clever escape from those situations is simply to stop and shoot what is cutely called a "minimaster," or a **pickup,** and move on. That way, not *everybody* on the set will know you have given up all hope of ever getting it right in one take. All right, a few, but not *everybody*.

Note: Despite seemingly contrary advice, it's often good practice to shoot one more master after you're happy with the printed one, this time as fast as possible. A simple direction to the actors should suffice: "Faster." You'll be glad you did it, and so will your editor. This is especially important when shooting a **one-er.**

matching The necessity to recreate or mimic the action from shot to shot, scene to scene. If a car moves right to left today, it must move right to left two months from now. If an actor takes a drink while saying a line in one angle, it's necessary to do it that way an hour—or a week—later when saying the same line in another shot. It's the job of the **script supervisor** to remind the actor (or more politely, the director) of the exact coordination required.

McGarrett A 50 mm lens, nicknamed for the character played by Jack Lord in the TV series *Hawaii Five-O*. An alternative term for the **Jack Lord.**

meal penalty A fine paid to the cast and crew, accruing in ten- or fifteen-minute increments, resulting from the failure to break for lunch in a timely manner (usually after six hours of work). In truth, it's usually not very expensive and should be only marginally considered when deciding whether to finish shooting a scene or setup. The term seems designed mainly to strike fear in the director's heart, and is often invoked as if associated with the guillotine.

Warning: It will take *at least* twice as long to finish a shot or scene after lunch than it would have just before lunch.

meat axe A piece of black wood or board attached to the end of a pole, resembling a cleaver; used to create small shadows and sometimes to shade the camera lens.

medium Usually understood as a shot framed from roughly the belt line. On the set, never say "Give me a medium shot," just say "Give me a medium."

Mickey Rooney A short creep. In this context, a slow, brief dolly move. You might expect that the diminutive Rooney wasn't happy about this term, but legend has it that this description was coined on the set of *The Black Stallion* TV series and that Rooney didn't mind at all. The directorial request to the camera department should be "Give me a Mickey Rooney."

mise-en-scène *Never* use this term on a film set; it will mark you as an academic or a total dweeb. Plus, no one will know what you're talking about anyway.

mix To blend together all the audio tracks. Again, in this country, the mixing stage (that is, the room itself) is sometimes referred to as the dubbing stage.

Montana A shot framed up from across the middle of the chest. Derives from the name of the mountainous western state (Montaña is the Spanish word for mountain). (*See also* **two Ts.**)

M.O.S. A shot or scene filmed without recording sound; an event that, ironically, often seems to throw the sound department into an "Okay-but-you'll-be-sorry" snit.

Industry mythology has M.O.S. deriving from the request of a long-gone German-speaking director—variously identified as Erich von Stroheim, Josef von Sternberg, or Ernst Lubitsch—to film a scene "*mit out sprechen*" (without speaking) or "*mit out* sound."

I don't think so. There is a less colorful but vastly

more plausible origin for M.O.S.: In the early decades of sound, until the 1950s, the sound track was recorded on an optical rather than magnetic track (now always called the "mag track"). When film was delivered to the lab for processing with a blank sound track, it was noted that it was being sent **M**inus **O**ptical **S**tripe. Makes much more sense to me, although I understand the appeal of the apocryphal version.

most favored nations clause A phrase used in contracts to denote that a party will be afforded equal treatment to the best-compensated of the other parties—usually the producer or star. Often used in defining the profits for the participants, the size and placement of billing, or the caliber of dressing rooms, etc. The phrase is almost always truncated as "favored nations": "Are the actors' deals all favored nations?"

mouse The eraser for the **slate,** usually homemade, with a powder-puff body tied to a chalk tail. Another charming vestige of the Golden Age of Hollywood. Unhappily, like its flesh and blood brethren, utterly dispensable, and a soon-to-be-permanent victim of digital technology.

movie Thought this one was a no-brainer? Me too, until I checked it out. You might think this word needs neither definition nor origin, that its etymology has been established and understood forever—but you'd be wrong.

It took a long time for the term to be accepted. Experimental terms had been tried: Cinematograph,

Kinetoscope, nickelodeon, nickelette, theatorium—all misfits. In Germany, they tried *wandelbilder* (wandering pictures), *lichtbild*, and *lichtspiel* (light play). But by 1909, "movie" began to circulate in newspaper comic strips. It wasn't an easy assimilation.

As Terry Ramsaye, the early and preeminent film historian, wrote in 1926: "The motion picture world is unalterably opposed to the word *movie* in any relation whatsoever. It is considered an unworthy, slangy diminutive. The motion picture will have nothing of the diminutives. The word *movie* appears to have come into the folk-tongue out of the gamin life of either New York or Chicago about 1906–1907. It had its beginning in Smithfield Street, near Diamond Alley, in Pittsburgh during Thanksgiving week in 1905. By 1908 *movie* began to appear in the reports of social workers and contemporary newspaper accounts. To the remainder of the world the motion picture is generally the *cinema* or the *kinema,* as a result of the early European dominance of the art by the device known as the *Cinematographe.* The American-born word *film* is, however, tending to invade all the European languages."

Historical Note: Contrary to the popular assumption that color film was first developed somewhere in the middle of the twentieth century, it was actually successfully shot and projected in 1908. The new process, called Kinemacolor, was developed in England. It was the first time in the world that a motion picture in natural colors was put on the screen. Soon other screenings were held in Berlin, Paris, and all the capitals of Europe, as well as Madison Square Garden in New York. Projectors were installed in three hundred cinemas in England and almost sixty films were made. But when the head of the Kinemacolor company, Charles Urban, tried to interest the American film industry in his revolutionary technology, his offer was rebuffed. The black-and-white film process was making millions; color was strange, complicated, and speculative. Why rock the boat? (*See also* **cinema.**)

moving on The equivalent of "cut, print"—although it usually follows those two words. The order to the entire crew to move on to the next scene or set. Sort of the equivalent to a pat on the back, and it often feels like that to the crew, if not the director. The same announcement is also called a *new deal*.

Moving on from a two-shot to a close-up is called *moving in* or *punching in*.

Musco light A very powerful truck that contains a generator and telescopic arm capable of almost a hundred-foot extension with sixteen 6K lights able to be adjusted remotely. (*See also* **condor.**)

"You must yourself unto the destructive element submit."

—JOSEPH CONRAD, *LORD JIM*

Mailing It In

YOU DON'T GET telegrams anymore. E-mails, sure. Faxes, maybe. But no telegrams. It's just as well. It was bound to be from someone trying to make something look official. And it was probably going to be bad news. A death, a lawsuit, a threat, an invitation to an event that takes itself too seriously. You didn't want to get one. Which is probably why you don't anymore. But a few years back, I got a telegram.

"Watch for the jewels," it said, "coming in May." There was no signature, but it had come from San Francisco. I didn't know anyone in that city who might be pulling my leg, and besides, it was only February, so I forgot about it. At the beginning of March the next one arrived. "Don't forget the jewels. Watch for delivery in May." This one got my attention as well. But I have no interest in jewelry, and I certainly hadn't ordered any. Once again, there was no signature, no return address, no way to trace it. April arrived, and another telegram: "Only thirty days until May. Expect jewels on the twelfth." By now I figured that I was probably going to get some kind of junk jewelry in May, that I was probably on someone's errant mailing list: the gemological equivalent of Publishers Clearing House. But a few days later, another telegram arrived. "Delivery delayed. Wait until further notice."

Yeah, right. And I should hold my breath and count slowly to a billion while I waited. Although I still didn't get the joke, I figured that someday I would deduce it or it would be revealed to me, probably by one of the more vengeful victims of my own occasional but complex practical jokes. The weeks rolled by and I forgot all about the telegrams.

Then one day in June the receptionist buzzed me to say that there was a guy at her desk with a package for me. I was busy, so I asked her to tell him to leave it with her. Long pause. "He says he can't. You have to sign for it. In person."

So I get up from my desk, walk down the hall, around the corner, and standing there I see not one but two messengers. Very official. In dark-blue security uniforms. Armed. One of them has a briefcase at his side. But not just any old banker's Naugahyde job—this one is made out of mahogany, varnished, and handcuffed to his wrists. "Are you Tony Bill?" he asks.

"No," I'm thinking, "the receptionist buzzed someone else, and I was hiding back there all morning just so I could jump out and impersonate myself." Thought it, didn't say it. Wimped out and just said, "Yes."

"Can I see some ID?" says the one without the attaché case. "Wait a minute. You know my address. You come in and ask for me. The receptionist calls me, I leave what I'm doing, walk down the hall, tell you who I am, and now you want my *ID*?"

Didn't say that either. Wimped out again and politely, if not cheerfully, pulled out my wallet, waited for The Man while he gave the up-down to my face and photo, then nodded to his partner-in-chains, who hefted the briefcase. Out came the keys—you know the drill, a ring with a couple dozen or so—and off came the cuffs. A rub of the wrist, a mumbled thanks, and they were gone. On the desk lay the shiny wood case; handmade, if I had to guess.

Beats there a heart so jaded among you, dear readers, breathes there a soul so cold that it could leave that briefcase unexamined? I doubt it. So I will spare you further suspense and tell you that I opened it there and then, and inside found nestled not jewels, of course, but two freshly minted scripts. They were from a writer unknown to me, un-agented, but, most important, audacious. I don't remember running back to my office and canceling the rest of my day to read the scripts, but you can bet that I did read them. And I'd bet you would, too. And so would any producer, director, or actor I can think of.

I'm afraid there's no happy ending to the story, except the one the writer intended: The scripts got read. And by the person to whom they were sent. That they did not, unfortunately, live up to their clever presentation is not the point here.

I have scant patience with the lament of writers who claim they cannot get someone to read their script. Instead, I'd offer that a clever-enough submission can get anyone to read (or rather, start to read) a script. (Okay, I know a lot of heavyweights employ a team of readers, but so what? That's their problem. If a reader reads your wonderful script first then passes it on to Mr. or Ms. Big, so be it. That's the way it's supposed to work. Of course, if it's not a wonderful script, you're wasting your time and theirs anyway.)

> I'm opinionated enough to say that anyone who can't figure out an original, imaginative, and fresh way of submitting a script probably doesn't have what it takes to write one.

In fact, I'm opinionated enough to say that anyone who can't figure out an original, imaginative, and fresh way of submitting a script probably doesn't have what it takes to write one. Granted, there's a fine line between audacious and annoying. But the same can be said of writing itself.

I've been amazed over the years at how seldom the imaginative or audacious submission is employed. There's something to be said for the normal, plain brown wrapper, to-whom-it-may-concern approach, but that something is BORING. Inevitably the accompanying script is in the same league. But let me share with you a few of the other approaches I've come across over the years, and see what you think.

The first really clever submission I ever heard of was on the first film I acted in, *Come Blow Your Horn*. Bud Yorkin and Norman Lear were a fledgling director/producer team with a few well-received television specials behind them. They had never made a movie. Frank Sinatra was arguably the biggest star in the world. And they desperately wanted him to read their script.

So one day a moving van pulled up to Mr. Sinatra's house. Out of this van, the men from Bekins unloaded a comfy leather armchair, a reading lamp, a bottle of Jack Daniel's, and—you guessed it—a script. Now Mr. Sinatra, big star or not, had a great sense of humor and an appreciation for audacity (you don't usually get that far without those qualities). And, as the saying goes, he put his pants on one leg at a time. So he started to read that script—just like anybody else would. After the first page, he and, more importantly, the script were on their own, one page at a time. That's how it has to work anyway. No amount of fancy footwork will counter a bad read. But it wasn't a bad read, it was a good one. And the rest is the history of a lot of people, including this writer.

I'm not above employing the art of surprise myself. A few years ago, my wife and producing partner, Helen Bartlett, had a project she was in love with. *Come and Go, Molly Snow* was a book about a female bluegrass fiddle player. The story was a powerful one, but in a rock 'n' roll, rap-centered marketplace, how could she convince a studio of the appeal of bluegrass music? Mike Marcus, the head of MGM, was at best cool to bluegrass. Assuming that the rest of the world reflected his own lack of exposure and enthusiasm, he had shown little interest in the book. Undaunted, Helen set up a meeting with him for us to try to sway him. Fifteen minutes was all she asked for.

The day arrived. The appointed hour arrived. Mike's assistant opened the door to his office and in walked not the producers, but Vassar Clements, one of the best bluegrass fiddlers in America, and two other musicians. Before Mike could figure out what was happening, they started to play. Ten minutes later, they walked back out. Twenty minutes later, he bought the book for us.

Another time, someone sent me a script with a $100 bill and a note saying, in effect, "I know your time is valuable. And I'm sure that $100 won't cover the two hours it'll take to read this, but it's worth it to me because I believe in it so much." How's that for a confident submission to get your attention and pique your interest? I sent the money back with an A-for-effort note, and of course I read the script. Who wouldn't?

Anchored off Malibu one summer afternoon, I looked up from a card game to see someone swimming out toward my sailboat. I figured it to be a friend, but as he got closer, I saw it wasn't. It was a guy with a script in a plastic bag. Swear to God. He tossed it aboard and swam back to shore. I don't remember reading that one, although I most probably did. It stays in my mind only as one of the more surreal submissions, but not a particularly imaginative one. Bizarre doesn't mean clever in my book.

That's not to say the most mundane circumstances cannot lead to reader's heaven. I was killing time in a café one afternoon many years ago, minding my own business, reading something, and having a beer. In comes a guy I didn't particularly want to see. I knew him and was friendly toward him, but he always had some scheme up his sleeve, and I usually didn't have the patience to listen. I leaned into my reading. Too late—he made a beeline for me, and before I knew it, I was sitting with him and some young guy he had in tow. "This is Rob Thompson," he said. "He's new in town. Just got down from Seattle."

The best I could come up with was "Oh, really? What are you doing here?"

"I've just written my first script and I came down to L.A. here to sell it."

Reflexively, I stuck my foot in it. "Well, I'm a producer. If you want someone to read it, that's what I do for a living."

He went out to his car, opened the trunk, and came back with a script. I started to read it. I kept on reading it. It was called *Hearts of the West*. It remains to this day my favorite of the films I've produced.

Not all overtures like that are promising; some require a bit of audacity on the part of the respondent. I think the most unlikely introduction to a writer came when I got a call from someone I had last seen in grammar school. I hardly knew him then, so you can imagine how unexcited I was to hear from him twenty-five years later. He was calling me from

Washington, D.C., he said, because he was with the government, and in a few days they were going to tear down a building somewhere in Virginia, and did I need a great location for my next film. Maybe I could shoot it now and use it later. His astounding naïveté notwithstanding, I carefully explained that we don't choose locations until we need them. And, oh, yeah, he added, "My brother-in-law just wrote his first script, and I wonder if you could read it and give him some advice."

His brother-in-law? Now, I'm a confessed sucker for an offbeat pitch, and I like to think I've always had a weather eye cocked for a clever submission, but the potential of this one augured for a less than promising grade, considering the source. Nevertheless, I bit. The script was terrific. I called the writer, reached him at an Indian restaurant in Washington where he was a waiter. Told him that if he'd rather write scripts than wait tables, I'd give him a round-trip ticket (coach) to L.A., a place to live, and enough to get by on. He did, so I did. Even though we've never yet made a film together, Bobby De Laurentiis has been well and deservedly employed in the movie business ever since.

Another inauspicious but bold submission occurred years ago at a raucous prerace party at the San

Diego Yacht Club. A very nervous guy came up to me in the middle of the festivities and handed me a script.

"My name's Michael Kane. I heard that you read scripts from unknown writers," he said. "Well, I'm one, and this is my first script, and I wonder if maybe you'd have time to read it on the race?" It was a weeklong race from San Diego to Puerto Vallarta, Mexico, so I guessed I would have time and I took it along. I loved it. When I got home, I called and asked him about himself. He had his own business, delivering soft drinks to Mexican communities in Los Angeles. His girlfriend had invited him to San Diego for the race party, and somehow he had heard that my boat was in the race. Michael had written the script in his stand-up delivery van during his daily route at stoplights and traffic jams. I bought him out of his soda business for a year and got him an agent, and he wrote the script for the first thing I ever directed—a film of O. Henry's classic "The Ransom of Red Chief." He's been writing fine screenplays ever since.

The Big Casino of show business operates on roughly the same, albeit less calculated, odds as Las Vegas. You can sit at the table for years, or you can hit the jackpot on your first hand. An agent once sent me a script when I was just starting to produce. I liked it a lot, but I thought it was only marginally producible.

Too offbeat. Still, I wanted to meet the author. He came to see me at my office, where I was trying to recover from the miserable failure of my first production; the very first offbeat script by a young man from Texas named Terry Malick. (I had made the two biggest mistakes a producer can make: hired the wrong director and didn't fire him.) So I asked this young writer, just out of UCLA, what he wanted to write next. He gave me about a five-minute sketch of an idea that I loved. Then, as now, I hated treatments or outlines, so I asked him to repeat it for me, on tape. Looking for an investor to help me develop it, I played it for a few apparently deaf ears until I came upon Julia and Michael Phillips. They had never produced a film; Michael wasn't even in the movie business. We commissioned the writer to deliver a script based on his verbal pitch, then waited almost two years without reading a word. He hadn't even told us the ending, saying only that it would be a surprise. It was. His name was David Ward. His script was titled *The Sting*.

While we were at it, we optioned his other offbeat, "marginally producible" script. And while we were waiting for those two years, we got it made. It was *Steelyard Blues*.

More recently my wife and I were at a New York

wedding party. In the middle of the festive dinner, a waiter came to our table to serve the vegetables. As he leaned over my shoulder, he whispered, "I've written a really great script."

"Good for you," I said. "Send it along. I'll read it. That's what I do for a living."

It wasn't a show-business wedding, so I wondered how in the world he'd picked me out of the crowd. And, of the random dozen of possibilities, how had he so cleverly contrived to be stationed at my table? I gave him high points for audacity, and frankly, as this was in Manhattan, I was not a little flattered to be so recognized.

"How do I get it to you?" he continued.

"I'm in the phone book in Venice."

I felt that little thrill of anticipation that I always feel when a writer has singled me out, when I think the script god has smiled on me again, that maybe This Could Be the One.

"Okay," he said. "What's your name?"

There is, of course, a downside to the unortho-

> When all else (including your imagination) fails, there is one method of submission that seldom fails to elicit at least attention, if not a response. And that's a terrific letter.

dox approach: embarrassment or failure. But so what? Isn't that the risk of anything that's fresh and imaginative? Certainly, there's that aforementioned fine line between audacious and obnoxious, but if you haven't the taste to discern it, and if you don't have the nerve to chance it, you're sunk anyway. I've been surprised at how few really imaginative submissions have even been attempted, much less backfired. It isn't so much a lost art as an undeveloped one.

When all else (including your imagination) fails, there is one method of submission that seldom fails to elicit at least attention, if not a response. And that's a terrific letter. Not a form letter. Not a To-Whom-It-May-Concern, Dear Madam, Dear Sir letter. Not a fax or an e-mail, either. (I hate to give away trade secrets, but I'd even eschew letters sent via the U.S. Mail. Why not a messenger-delivered letter? It smacks of two things: class and importance.) As far as I know there is one thing that presidents and popes, rock stars and movie stars all have in common: They read their mail. And somehow, the grabbers—the passionate, bold, imaginative letters—get their attention. Write one. You'll be surprised. And you probably won't be the only one.

Navajo blanket A rusty wire scrim—so rusty that it is like "putting a blanket in front of the light."

N.D. Nondescript. Most often used to describe cars or extras needed for background. One doesn't normally ask for N.D. statues or N.D. airplanes, for example, but it could happen. N.D. dogs and N.D. cows are a possibility, but it would usually be redundant.

Ambiguity Alert: This term can also refer to the camera department's neutral density filters or gels, used to **knock down** or balance background light, especially on windows.

N.G. No good, unusable, as in an incomplete or unacceptable take.

nine-iron Same as **broom it,** that is, get rid of it. "That's a nine-iron." Oddly, not derived directly from golf. It comes from the heyday of the western, where the long-handled pooper-scooper used to clean up after the horses was called a "nine-iron."

"no one knows anything" The oft-quoted observation of screenwriter William Goldman, who has written three or four good scripts, all but one (*Butch Cassidy and the Sundance Kid*) being adaptations of his or other writers' bestselling books (*Marathon Man, Misery, All the President's Men*)—and about twenty mediocre-to-worse ones. The quotation, like a lot of his work, is facile and fun but fatuous.

"nobody moves, nobody gets hurt" The assistant director's way of saying "Quiet on the set." A punning reference to a million hackneyed bank-robbery scenes. Short on its ability to charm or amuse.

noncombatants Anyone not in the scene or not working at the time, usually crew. Normally heard when clearing the set for rehearsal or shooting. (*See also* **civilians.**)

norvalize To play an element (sound effect, music, dialogue) so low that, although present, it basically can't be heard. A vain attempt to hide the fact that it is not in sync. Named for the sound editor Norval Crutcher, who had a penchant for mixing thus.

O

obie A small light mounted on the camera just over the lens. Named for Merle Oberon, the beautiful actress whose famous eyes it was invented for. The inventor was her husband, the legendary cameraman Lucien Ballard. (A notoriously imperious and dictatorial character, Ballard carried a riding crop on the set and used it to point out the placement of lights and, with equal effect, to prod his crew.)

Without Obie

With Obie

on the day Shorthand for "when we do it"—whether five minutes, five weeks, or even five seconds from now. As with **"good morning,"** film set-time is subjective, so "on the day" varies with the context. Thus: "On the day [three weeks from now] we'll have seventy-five extras" or "On the day [in the next scene] the gun will have a half-load."

on the floor On the editing room floor, that is. Describes footage being shot that is clearly a waste of time or is destined to be uncuttable. "This is only going to end up on the floor."

Caution: On the set, only directors are allowed to utter this kiss of death. For any other crewmember to make this (often obvious) observation is considered out of place and ill-mannered to the point of blasphemy.

Note: Despite ubiquitous use of the term, film, of course, no longer actually ends up on the editing room floor or anywhere else in the editing room, for that matter. Everyone edits digitally today, except a few holdouts who still prefer to edit the old-fashioned way (Steven Spielberg among them). Some complain that digital editing has made films more choppy due to the ease with which cuts may be effected. This may or may not be true. A more serious, and real, effect is that the digital revolution has eradicated the contemplative period between cuts and between screenings that was formerly an unavoidable part of the editorial process. Films can now be assembled in a few weeks and recut on a moment's notice or an executive's whim (*see also* **preview**). And because they can be, they are—especially under the pressure of studios to save money or meet long-held release dates. There's a lot to be said for the relatively leisurely pace at which editing once followed shooting. Movies were shot for weeks and edited for months. Those days are gone with the rewind. Now they're shot for months and edited in weeks.

on the lot Purists would hold that this only refers to the property owned by the major studios. As such, it is, if not endangered, at least an increasingly selective term. In the heyday of the major studios, all of them had a lot—with offices, prop, wardrobe, and camera departments, etc.—but also a back lot containing various permanent sets, such as a Western town, a New York street, a Midwestern neighborhood. The back lot of 20th Century Fox is now the high-rises of Century City; the back lot of MGM is currently condos; the back lot of Paramount has been eradicated, and Columbia's has disappeared (as has Columbia as a physical studio—it's now a part of Sony on the former MGM lot). Only Warner Bros. may truly claim what little is left of its back lot. The Universal back lot is really just a relic, used mainly as a tourist attraction, a shell of a shell.

on the mag To dolly in the direction of the film magazine, that is, straight ahead.

one-er A scene shot in one continuous shot, neither requiring nor accommodating any further **coverage.** Why waste a cut when one shot will do? One-ers can be as simple as two people sitting (the final scenes of Mike Nichols' *The Birdcage* and *The Graduate*; Ratso's death in *Midnight Cowboy*) or as complex as the brilliantly kinetic first half-dozen minutes of *The Player*, *Goodfellas*, or *Bound for Glory*.

Many of the most ambitious one-ers are the first scene of a film, as if, like an eager boxer, the first impression made by this fancy footwork will guarantee the next two hours' success. Conversely, they are favored final shots of many—if not most—films: the director's last hurrah. (Unforgettable: the last shot of *The 400 Blows*.) One-ers are at their finest when they are graceful and unobtrusive. Not all of them are flamboyant, elaborate, or close up. Some are just quietly daring, and the camera doesn't move at all.

One-ers can basically be divided into what I would call "the show-off" (where the director is doing just that) and "the bail-out." The bail-out is used often in television and can be called upon to save the director's skin even under the most dire circumstances. It's hard to commit to the bail-out early in the day (*see* **GWTW**), but after lunch, when you're running behind and looking over your shoulder, it is the Superman of shots—able to stop that speeding train of time in a single shot.

One of my favorite one-ers: the office scene in *The Verdict* in which Paul Newman gets the telephone call. Another is the daring last scene of *Big Night*. Or check out some of Woody Allen's movies (especially

One-er

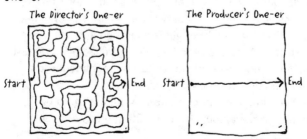

The Director's One-er

Start — End

The Producer's One-er

Start — End

those shot by Gordon Willis) where the actors walk off-camera during the scene. Or Liza Minnelli's phone call in *The Sterile Cuckoo*. You could call all these the **lock-off** one-er. The **CGI** revolution has made all sorts of previously impossible one-ers commonplace. (Watch the last, incredibly moving shot of Clint Eastwood's *Space Cowboys*—it's a movie in itself.)

Among the most famous one-ers is Jean-Luc Godard's ten-minute shot in *Week End* in which a couple is stranded in a traffic jam, as well as Mikhail Kalatozov's acrobatic shot in 1964's *I am Cuba* and Michelangelo Antonioni's *The Passenger*. The latest installments in the canon include scenes in *Atonement* and *Children of Men*.

A.D.'s love a one-er because it invites them to marshal all those years of training and experience and really shine. (A.D.'s like to show off, too.) In bail-out mode, it saves them from the lashes of blame sure to be given them by everyone (including the director) for not having scheduled the day properly.

Script supervisors and actors generally love the one-er too, as it relieves them of the constraints of matching dialogue or action. The exception is the actor who panics when learning that a one-er is in the works and shoulders the weight of getting through a whole scene perfectly. If the desire to be good is the actor's greatest enemy—and it is—the one-er can be tantamount to a final audition or an opening night.

The filmed length of a one-er would seem to be limited to the amount of film a 35 mm camera could hold (a thousand feet, or about five-and-a-half minutes), but the video revolution has rendered that limit moot and apparently infinite. *The Russian Ark* (2002) is the longest one-er in history—a 99-minute **feature** consisting of a single (hi-def) **Steadicam** shot. Amazing. The opening title sequence of *Touch of Evil* and Hitchcock's whole movie *Rope* are considered two of the most famous one-ers ever. Except—look again—*Rope* isn't *really* a one-er.

Warning: Undertaking the one-er can be an invitation to disaster. Several cautions apply:

1. Try not to announce your intention to shoot a one-er. Once a one-er is perceived by anyone on the set to be in the making, word will spread like wildfire and an early (or at least earlier) end to the day will be expected. The comedown from this high can be nasty.

2. Once you've gotten a really good one-er, seriously consider walking away. The second attempt will take two to ten times as long to get right again (if ever), has only a 50 percent chance (at most) of being better, and will probably erase all the time you saved. (*See also* **one for safety.**)

3. At some point in your efforts, be prepared to abandon the whole concept and fall back on a conventional method of covering the scene. (*See also* **pickup; insert.**) Confess this to your A.D. early and confidently.

Although the snappy name owes nothing to the one-night stand, the same decision-making question should be applied: "Will I hate myself in the morning?"

one for safety An extra take of the same shot just printed, made in the illogical hope that some imagined ruination of the printed shot will not also befall the safety shot. The motion picture equivalent of grandma taking one more photo of the kids from the same vantage point, one for safety is usually a waste of time and often a lot of it. A more legitimate—and frequent—reason would be a concern if something were out of focus.

open up To turn slightly toward the camera. It's not uncommon for a director or camera operator to ask an actor to "open up" just a bit: to favor the camera in a scene where they would otherwise have their back or profile to camera.

Warning: Some actors will take great offense at this slightly artificial directorial request. (*See also* **cheat.**) Unfortunately, the only way to find out who they are is to ask them someday to "open up."

outtakes Unused takes that have been printed but not used.

over A shot over the back shoulder of one actor onto the face another. Sometimes called an *over-shoulder*. Clever actors, vying for the most audience contact possible will sometimes play to the closer-to-camera eye of their partner, giving the somewhat spaced-out impression of what in Vietnam was called *the thousand-yard stare*. It is not nearly as cool to say "Give me an over-the-shoulder shot" as it is to say "Give me an over."

Another kind of over would be from the front of two actors talking side by side; a *reverse over* would be shot from behind them.

Over

Over the shoulder   Over the counter   Over my dead body

P.A. Production Assistant. The bottom rung of the crew positions, yet a coveted one. This is the lowest- (and often, non-) paying job on the set, with the longest hours and least appreciation. Not a union position, it's usually filled by students, neighbors, relatives, and hopeful filmmakers looking for a toe in the door. And the work is not even guaranteed to be on the set: it may be back at the production office, copying pages; standing in a street all night to protect some parking spaces; bringing coffee to the director. On non-union movies, it could be *driving* the director. It's the movie equivalent of the circus worker who cleans up after the elephants ("What? And quit show business?"). Ask around: It's where many, many people got their start. It's not beneath you; go for it.

Paganinis In England: a series of boxes of varying height used to stabilize chairs, props, etc., and, on occasion, the camera. The name would appear to have something to do with the great Italian violinist Niccolò Paganini, but his connection to these boxes is lost to history. Often called *pags*.

pan A slow side to side, left to right, or right to left movement of the camera about its own axis. A fast one is called a swish pan or a whip pan. Logically, you cannot pan up or down (*see also* **tilt**), although more than a few naive directors have requested this.

pancake If you thought this was body makeup, go back to film school. **Apple boxes** have little flat cousins, usually used to boost an actor, and they are called **pancakes.** (*See also* **manmaker.**) Body makeup, by the way, is called body makeup.

pay or play A guarantee to pay the actor, director, producer, etc., regardless of whether or not the movie gets made—or if they get replaced. Next to "check enclosed," the most welcome expression in the movie business. This commitment, once made—even on the phone—is binding and honored throughout the industry.

peanut The smallest **inky.**

perms High up, around the periphery of the soundstage, are the wooden walkways referred to as the perms. Suspended from them are other walkways and catwalks called greenbeds. The latter term refers to the color these were almost always painted, although the reason for that color is unclear. The space between these walkways is called the ozone.

Perrier meeting A meeting that lasts only until one's water glass is empty.

pickup A decision, often uttered through clenched teeth, to start shooting an angle or scene again from a point of interruption, usually after it is clear to everyone on the set that it will be impossible to shoot from beginning to end as written. The salvation of actors who can't remember their lines or have trouble sustaining a performance, and often the salvation of the director whose take has been interrupted by a passing airplane or some such. Also very useful as a directorial sop to actors and producers asking for another whole take when all that really bothered them was a certain moment.

Two schools of thought prevail: The more disparaging is that the pickup is a production shortcut, a kind of cheap, patchwork approach to filmmaking. It is, for example, used a lot in television production. The other school says that it's the mark of a canny director, who knows and shoots only what is really needed. ("That's a print and a pickup.") Both schools are correct.

Note: The pickup is the tool of choice to salvage the flailing or moribund **one-er**. You'll usually need only a simple cutaway to jump back in the scene.

piece of business An actor's gesture or action, sometimes suggested by the director, to make them appear naturally engrossed, even if not directly relating to the scene. Lighting a cigarette, fumbling for a wallet, or looking through a book would be a piece of business. Often the director will ask the **A.D.** to give an extra a piece of business to make them appear lifelike instead of zombielike.

pirate ship To make a copy of a sound effect for one's own library. Not heard often, and too bad. Used to refer to making a copy of good sound effects recorded in production; thus the request to "pull up the pirate ship" is to make sure those recordings will be available after the film is finished and the masters are sent away. The sound of a car crash in today's movie may have been recorded twenty years ago.

Pirate ship

poor man's process A way of shooting a scene that eliminates the use of rear or front projection, or going on location to shoot a scene, typically inside a car, boat, airplane, train, etc. This is usually accomplished by preventing the audience from seeing outside the conveyance used, in daylight scenes by **blowing** out the windows; in night scenes, by a clever use of passing lights and shadows to give the illusion of motion. Actors are sometimes inclined to overdo the illusion, and you can often spot the use of poor man's by watching an actor driving, turning the wheel back and forth much more than anyone would if driving for real. (Airplane in-flight scenes used to be shot this way, particularly badly, by blowing some smoke past and shooting against a blue sky background while the actor/pilot moves the stick like he's stirring a large pot of soup. In fact, they often still are.) Usually abbreviated as *poor man's* or simply *P.M.P.*

Done well, the general audience never recognizes this **cheat;** it's much easier to shoot than actually driving or flying, and it's totally controllable. A lot of directors turn up their noses at this low-budget technique. They shouldn't.

pork chop A removable footrest, used on the dolly. Named for the cut of meat it resembles.

powder man An explosives expert.

practical Any light on a set seen on camera that actually belongs there, such as a reading lamp, a refrigerator light, or a dining-room chandelier. Some cinematographers have lit whole scenes with only the practicals.

Also, a **set** is either a practical or a **build.**

preview One of the final stages of filmmaking hell. Sometimes it's a free showing for the audience tacked on to the featured movie at the theater. Or it can be a *spill and fill*, where the theater is emptied out and then reopened to admissions. A particularly torturous form is the recruited preview, where an invited audience of the general public, usually approached at shopping malls and chummed with free tickets, is invited to pontificate on everything from the quality of the dialogue to the pace of the editing. The director is typically expected, and often ordered, to accommodate these opinions with ameliorating changes in the film. Most directors, appropriately, countenance these events with the anticipation of a Christian approaching lions.

To be precise, the *sneak preview* is a screening of the finished film shortly before the scheduled release date in order to build word-of-mouth anticipation.

Priscilla Silver lamé stretched on a frame, used to bounce light.

producer Traditionally a poorly dressed, ambitious, egocentric, overpaid, inexperienced newcomer, usually imagined with a starlet and a cigar. The director, on the other hand, was expected to be mature in demeanor, if not in years, well-mannered, struggling, dedicated, poorly paid, and long-suffering.

Over the past few decades, this situation has become reversed.

Also traditionally expected was that the director would come up the hard way, earning stripes first in the more lowly depths of the movie business food chain, perhaps the theater, often as an actor. The producer could be any schmo off the street with an attitude and an ego big enough to hide his inexperience.

In fact, these definitions may be considered obsolete, except insofar as they now apply to their opposites. Producers, by and large, do not get rich and, with a few notable exceptions—most of them dead or sequestered in rehab—do not behave outrageously. (By industry agreement, there are no more than fifteen really rich producers alive at any one time.) The vast majority of producers, contrary to their stereotypical portrayals, do not actually spend their own money on the production of films; they spend other people's money, assembling it from studios, foreign sales, DVD rights, and other sources.

A subset known as the creative producer is an endangered species. The concept behind this rara avis used to be that the creative producer had an idea, risked his own money in acquiring and developing it, hired the writer, director, and star(s), and was the guiding force, if not the final word, in the making and marketing of the film. Often these producers were responsible for the best films of their directors' careers, and such was the weight of this contribution that the creative producer actually *deserved* a possessive credit, as in "A Jerry Hellman Production," "A Sam Spiegel Picture," or "A Saul Zaentz Production."

There's also the line producer. That's the person charged by the studio or the producer with seeing to it that everything runs smoothly on the set and that the film comes in on budget. You'd think this would normally be part of the producer's job, but sometimes it's eschewed and sometimes, especially on big-budget films, it requires a very high degree of experience and expertise.

Producing is arguably the worst, most frustrating job in the movie business. Once, I was standing nearby when producer Harry Gittes (*Goin' South, About Schmidt,* and the namesake for Jack Nicholson's character in *Chinatown*) was talking on the phone, trying to put a movie deal together. As he slammed down the receiver, I heard him shout to himself, "Jesus Christ! You have to fight to get into the fucking war!" That's the most accurate definition of producing I have ever heard.

I think the most common **civilian** question asked about life on the set is something like "What's the difference between what a producer does and what a director does?" While nothing in the **real world** comes very close to that delicate balance of power and creative control that exists on the set, there's one parallel that comes close: in football, the relationship between the coach (producer) and the quarterback (director).

They're both there at the pleasure of an owner/financier; they both have to pull together a team and efficiently guide it to success; they both know the game. Coach hires quarterback, stays on the sidelines; quarterback's on the field with the team, carrying the ball. The coach might call the plays some or most of the time, or the quarterback might. The coach can fire the quarterback; the quarterback can override the coach . . . depending on who they are. Sometimes the coach fires the q'back, sometimes . . . well this could

go on and on, but I think you get the drift. (*See also*
associate producer.)

production designer A mid-twentieth-century
moniker. Before that it was called the Art Director.
There was a set designer, a set decorator, a costume
designer; perhaps even a hair or costume designer.
There still are those categories, but now there is an all-
inclusive position; elevated and distinguished, as well
as expanded. The production designer is responsible
for coordinating all aspects of the visual imagery of a
film: cinematography, costume, makeup, location, color
selections, architecture, set design, etc.

   The term was created in 1939 to describe the many
contributions of William Cameron Menzies on *Gone with
the Wind.*

pull the plug Usually used as a warning to the director
that the producer or production manager is prepared to
terminate the day's shooting—which may be going into

Pull the plug

golden time. "We're gonna pull the plug" is about the only solution left when the shooting day has dragged on and on. Usually tinged with the slight aura of a threat.

pup Any small light.

pushcart A code word among the crew to notify each other of a woman on the set who is sitting in such a manner that one might see up her dress.

put some iron on the chain To add a processing device to affect the sound during the mix.

raintree A very tall sprinkler used, normally in multiples, to simulate rain. Virtually all rain in movies is created this way. In fact, rain doesn't show up on film unless it is carefully backlit. Like a cop, it's never there when you need it and often there when you don't.

real world As sailors differentiate between being at sea or at land; as prisoners view life outside their walls; as the military sees civilians; so does the film crew differentiate life on the set from life off the set . . . which they call, not altogether dismissively, the real world.

rear projection The projection of a scene (highway, ski slope, surf, passing scenery, etc.) behind the actor(s) during a scene to give the illusion that they are really there, driving, skiing, surfing, etc.

The scene projected is called, oddly, a *plate*, though it's obviously a moving image. (*Plate* may be a holdover from the earliest days of cinema, when it was not necessary for the background to be a motion picture, only a photograph.)

Rear projection is virtually extinct, replaced by front projection. Again, it's a form of **cheat** that goes right by the audience, although both forms have been generally replaced by **CGI** techniques, which are virtually impossible to distinguish from the real thing.

recce The British word for the **location scout,** derived from "reconnaissance," although sounding to American ears more like a Girl Scout field trip.

redhead An open-faced 1K light. Also called a *mickey*.

Rembrandt The generic but well-earned moniker given to the key on-set (or standby) painter. Long on the endangered species list, this term may now be considered virtually extinct. The cry of "Rembrandt!" was once all the prompting necessary to summon this paint-spattered (and seemingly oldest) member of the crew, who would quietly and instantly appear, bucket and brushes in hand, like a country doctor making a house call. It was rare to know the real name of this magician. Imagine, by the way, the lost charm of hearing "Good morning, Rembrandt" every day.

Rembrandt

You missed a spot.

Rembrandt lighting A lighting style that dramatically emphasizes a few aspects of the subject while letting the rest of the scene go very dark. Named for the style of the painter, it's created by placing the key light at a horizontal angle of forty-five degrees with the vertical angle approximately the same.

reshoot A scene or shot redone after it has been originally shot. Also referred to as a *retake*. Usually a posteditorial event after it becomes evident that a scene or a performance can be improved upon. A new ending or a new scene, however, is not technically a reshoot but an added scene. It's not unusual for films to reshoot or add many scenes, but it is often taken to imply a film in trouble. However, the "trouble" is often cured by the added or reshot scenes. Woody Allen has an interesting, albeit privileged, approach to filming: He builds into every budget a couple of weeks of additional shooting, followed by another week or so of yet more filming. He once reshot an *entire film* (*Mighty Aphrodite*).

rhubarb Gibberish, or generic dialogue, requested of extras by the **A.D.** to avoid paying them as actors with written lines. The postproduction equivalent is **walla**.

Ritters Large industrial fans used on set to create strong winds, often powered by automobile or aircraft engines. Named after the famous singing cowboy Tex Ritter, who was once blown off his saddle by one. Just kidding: They were named by their inventor, Art Fritzen, of the California Fritzen Propeller Company.

room tone The ambient sound present on the actual set or location, indoors or out. The sound department is always anxious to record this even though it's usually endured by the crew as optional and a nuisance. But it's always worth the extra few minutes it takes to record it at the end of a completed scene. The filmmaking equivalent of not forgetting to take your vitamins; later on, you'll be glad you did.

rough cut The first edited viewing of the film, usually after the self-descriptive assemblage. Watching the rough cut is best left to the director and editor. Others may be invited, but this is usually a big mistake. It is axiomatic that no director can enjoy this experience. Nor, most likely, can anyone else. Anyone who claims to love a rough cut is probably lying or toadying. Conversely, anyone who hates a rough cut and talks about it is liable to eat their words later. The bragging rights attendant with having judged someone else's rough cut are not worth the harm and embarrassment to the filmmakers or oneself that is sure to attend the final version, be it evolved for better or worse. Discretion, one of the film industry's scarcest commodities, is always in order here.

roundy-roundy Same as turning around, i.e., reversing the camera direction, but much more chipper, sometimes annoyingly so. I once heard of an **A.D.** who was fired for announcing "Roundy-roundy on the tomato" (meaning "the actress"). (*See also* **do-si-do.**)

rubber Slang for latex makeup or special effects.

run 'n' gun To shoot very quickly. Often synonymous with low-budget techniques.

rushes *See* **dailies.**

sandbag Sandbags are ubiquitous on movie sets. Usually fifteen pounds, they are used for stabilizing **C-stands,** marking actors' positions, and all sorts of improvised purposes. They're also known as *silent grips*. The thirty-five-pounders are sometimes called *ballbusters*.

script About 120 pieces of paper or less, upon which is written a vivid, succinct description of a movie that might or might not have been made.

Scripts are also known as *screenplays*. It's a close call, but use of that word seems a bit more highfalutin' these days and is used mostly in print, for credits, awards, and reviews. Screenplay is actually a derivative of *photoplay*. In 1912, the Essanay concern in Chicago, formed five years earlier by Max Aronson (later G. M. Aronson), star of *The Great Train Robbery,* and George K. Spoor, offered the world a prize of twenty-five dollars for a new name for the movie writer's art. Edgar Strakosch, a California musician, coined *photoplay* and got the money. Within a few months, *Photoplay Magazine* was founded in Chicago and spread the word to the industry and the public.

script supervisor The person responsible for: timing the script before and during production; keeping track of the **continuity** (hour, day, month, year, etc.); screen direction (*see also* **split looks**); character logic; **matching;** and a whole slew of other technical aspects of the day. This is easily the most complex and complicated position on the set—although one which script supervisors themselves treat as if it's no big deal.

Before the 1970s, this position used to be called the *script girl* because traditionally the job was filled by a woman; probably the only one thus defined on the set. It still pretty much is, although there are some fine male script supervisors. But not many. Note that there are no "script boys," just as there are no "best girls" (*see also* **best boy**).

I've always been fascinated by one curious and common quirk of this crew position: the words virtually all of them use to indicate the alphabet, when numbering takes. You would think they'd use the universally understood International Alphabet: Alpha, Bravo, Charlie, Delta, Echo, Foxtrot . . . etc. But they don't; they have their own hybrid of it: Apple, Biker, Charlie, Edward, Frank, George, Henry; after that, they improve or customize with crewmembers' names. No one knows how this came to pass, or why it persists.

First-time Director Advice: If you do nothing else to help yourself through the challenges that await you, look for the kindest, most experienced, most skilled script supervisor available.

seagull Any generic, meaningless cutaway. Derived from the countless movies in which seagulls were used to cut away to, regardless of their relationship to the scene (or story). The concept can be anything you want as long as you get away with it: a sunset, kids playing, time-lapse clouds. Often thought of as an editorial Band-Aid, because that's what it usually is. A poor cousin to the **insert.**

Seagull

second unit An additional crew, including a **director** and **D.P.,** assigned to shoot scenes or shots that do not require the director or the **stars** of a film. They might work concurrently with the main unit, in postproduction, on a distant **location,** or on an effects (or green screen) stage.

A kissin' cousin is the *splinter unit:* crewmembers culled and sent off to shoot while the rest of the main unit continues to work. This usually happens on or very near the main unit shooting.

set The larger definition is synonymous with the stage where filming is taking place and includes all the sets thereon. Understood to be a man-made place (bathroom, office, restaurant, etc.), usually at the studio. On the microcosmic level, can be interior or exterior. Apart from the models and the **CGI** work, most of the *Titanic* was a set. A set dressed and waiting to be used is labeled a "hot set," with the (obvious) understanding that it is not to be touched.

The opposite of a set is a location; however, once a location is in use, it becomes known as the set. To further confuse the uninitiated: Although one may also build a set on a location, there is really no such term as a *location set*. Thus, one can be "at the location" and still be either on or off the set.

Any movie-related communication may be accomplished by asking the **A.D.**s (usually the second A.D.) for the use of the set phone, although the ubiquity of cell phones has made this item almost obsolete.

It wasn't always so easy. In the early days, shooting in the desert or other remote locations outside of Los Angeles was hampered by the lack of not only cell phones, of course, but also by the absence of pay phones. Film companies let the studio know of their progress or problems through the use of homing pigeons, which were able to be back in Hollywood within an hour or so.

set piece A scene that's more complex and elaborate than most of the other scenes; usually remembered long after the plot is forgotten. Often a stand-alone sequence requiring no introduction. It can be an action sequence, a particularly dramatic or comedic scene. There is a credible theory, bruited about in the screenwriting community, that a movie needs at least three or four set pieces in order to "work" or succeed. This bit of popular wisdom, like most, is both suspect and substantive. Set pieces make prime candidates for **trailers.** The bar scene in *Star Wars* is a good example.

sheet metal A car in car commercials. Used mainly to describe that category of commercials and/or the directors who specialize in filming cars and making them look as good as possible.

shoe leather A pejorative term for shots, or even scenes—usually without dialogue—that serve only to move characters geographically, as in walking up to a house, getting on an airplane, etc. Dialing a phone, getting dressed, paying the taxi driver, and other time-consuming actions may also qualify as "just shoe leather."

shoot Of course, everyone knows that this means to point a camera at something or someone and to turn it on. But did you know that it derives from the period when cameramen first aimed the camera then turned the crank, like a machine gun? That's the likely derivation of the word. "Gun it!" was the early-twentieth-century director's command to the cameraman when starting to film.

short ends The various lengths of unexposed film left

over after shooting. It's seldom possible to expose exactly the amount of film in the magazine, so the unused lengths are saved for reuse on the production or sold to companies that recycle them for cheap use on other productions (or 35 mm still cameras). Student films and very low-budget features are often made entirely with short ends.

showcard A piece of white artist's cardboard used as a reflector.

shower curtain A large, translucent plastic sheet used to soften lights.

sides Rather than tote around the whole script, actors and crew are given **sides**—the few pages of the script, reduced in size, that they are shooting that day. Sides are also used for auditions, when actors are reading just a few scenes.

silver bullet A 12K or 18K light manufactured by the Cinemills Corp.

single Any shot with only one actor in the frame. Generally a fairly close shot, but not necessarily a close-up.

slam cut A misnomer of a misnomer. A mercifully rare variant of **smash cut.**

slate The clapper board on which the name of the production, the date, and the number of the scene are written. Originally marked in chalk—hence the name, as a chalkboard is made of and called a slate. (More common these days is a plastic board with erasable marker.)

In a bow to tradition, the slate also displays the name of the director and cinematographer—as if anyone watching dailies needs to be reminded. Many people do not know what the clapper, or stick, is there for: Its purpose is to give the editor an audible and visual cue with which to synchronize the sound and picture tracks.

Originally this synchronizing device was simply two pieces of wood clapped together. The ritual was considered so important that it was the director's prerogative to do

it. He would roll the camera, announce the scene number, clap the sticks together, then zip back behind the camera and call the action. Small wonder that the job was soon relegated to the camera assistant, with whom it remains.

smash cut A very commonly mis- and overused term, usually affected by second-rate screenwriters trying to spice up otherwise pedestrian writing. The same goes for **slam cut** and **crash cut**—bastards all. The great screenwriter Ernest Lehman (*North by Northwest, Sabrina, The King and I*) used the term *shock cut* only *once* in his script of *West Side Story*, but then *he was Ernest Lehman*. Generally, a cut is a cut is a cut; theoretically, a smash cut is a cut from a still or quiet environment to a shockingly active or noisy one. On the printed page, it is invariably a sign of straining amateurism.

Advice to Screenwriters: Never use it.

smoke The cinematographer's best friend. Smoke is often used to diffuse the light in a scene or set, but also to create visible beams of light. Sure, it will look, well, smoky on the set, but—used judiciously—this technique is usually invisible to the audience's eye.

snot tape Clear, two-sided tape, usually used for gels, nets, etc., and when rolled up in a gooey little ball, worthy of its name.

snowshoes When someone trips over a wire, kicks a plug out, disturbs a light, etc., they may be asked to take off their snowshoes.

sound mixer The member of the sound crew responsible for recording all of the sounds and sound effects on a set. The delicate twirling and sliding of mysterious knobs attending this job smacks of brain surgery, but consider this: The legendary Oscar-winning sound man Nat Boxer (*The Conversation, Apocalypse Now,* and, lucky for me, *My Bodyguard*) was a **boom man.** He often traveled to location alone and picked up a local mixer. He claimed he could teach anyone to do the job in a day or so; the art of sound recording was the art of which mic to use and where to place and move it.

(Sorry, mixers of the world, that's what Nat said.)

soundstage A large, soundproof studio, usually with interior stages, used in a film production. At a major film company, the many soundstages resemble warehouse buildings and are numbered. Some numbers, such as seven and thirteen, are omitted for superstitious reasons.

sound track The sound for a film, strictly speaking, *not* the music in the film. Technically, the term should not be used to refer to the CD or other release of the music sold to the public, but it's clearly too late to enforce this.

soup The chemical bath used to develop the film at the **lab.** (Also referred to, naturally enough, as the bath.)

special effect On the set, the special effects department is responsible for the fire, smoke, squibs, explosions, and other mechanical and magical tricks of the trade.

Also understood to be a postproduction manipulation of the film; these days it's generally a **CGI** effect. Originally, the special effects department was called—much more appropriately, don't you think?—the trick department.

"speed!" The call from the production **sound mixer** signifying that the tape is rolling. The term is, in fact, an anachronism. Although it is universally assumed—even by most sound crews—that this means that the tape is "up to speed," this is erroneous. Modern recorders are up to speed almost the instant they are turned on, and certainly by the time the camera rolls. The term is a vestige of a much earlier technology; which one is open to question.

One theory has it that "speed" refers to the era of the hand-cranked camera, which had to be cranked up to the proper speed before the action began, and this was originally a camera operator's call. Another is that in early days of sound the camera was actually turned on by the sound department. The power supply in those days was DC current and had to be synchronized with the sound at 600 cycles per second, Thus, the sound department's call of speed to confirm that moment.

In any event, the mixer's call of "speed" today basically means simply that he is awake. . . . not always a self-evident assumption.

spider An electrical connector placed on the floor that accommodates several plugs.

spill Light falling where it is not intended or escaping from the sides of a lighting unit.

split looks This situation is so complex that it cannot be explained in words. (Much like trying to describe a spiral staircase without using one's hands.) And yet it is often the cause of much wasted time and contentious side-taking among the **D.P.,** director, **script supervisor,** camera crew, stars, and random other crewmembers, usually in that order. I have seen people virtually come to blows on a set arguing over resolving this seemingly innocuous issue. For example, scenes around a table are split-look magnets; so are classroom and courtroom scenes.

Basically, it is the dilemma that arises when one actor is speaking to two or more others and, in cutting from one to the other, the eyelines don't match. See? I told you—it's complicated.

Bottom line? Directors are well advised to stay out of these split looks skirmishes until absolutely certain that one side has made the most sensible argument, and even then to proceed cautiously. Better still, immediately announce that you'll shoot it both ways, thus saving time, on-set harmony—and face.

spo The optimum viewing spot in a theater. Always in the center and usually about halfway between the projection booth and the screen. Spo first came into usage during the mix of Francis Ford Coppola's *Apocalypse Now*. (To spoach is to arrive early at a movie theater and get the best seats for you and your yet-to-arrive friends. I think of it as a contraction of "seat poach." Intelligible only among members and graduates of Coppola's American Zoetrope, and not recommended outside those confines.)

spud The male attachment for a light.

squash and stretch Animation term for distorting a character in an elastic, rubbery effect.

squeezer A dimmer.

squib When you see bullets hitting cars, walls, doors, etc., those were not (one hopes) real bullets; they were squibs, little explosive packets carefully placed and wired to go off exactly on cue. The same with the actors; squibs are hidden inside their clothing.

stand-in A person of the (usually) same height, hair color, and skin color as the actor to be photographed, used on the set for lighting purposes. Not to be confused with a double, who looks enough like the actor (usually a star) to be photographed from a distance in the absence of the actor (such as during second unit photography). Movie stars usually have their favorite double—who is employed whenever the star works—as well as their favorite stunt double.

Stand-in

Star Stand-in Double Stunt double

star If golf is "a good walk spoiled," then a movie star is a normal human being essentially brainwashed. This Pavlovian treatment is administered daily and unconsciously by all of us, all of humanity, who read their interviews, laugh at their jokes, seat them at the best tables, keep them from waiting, tell them how great they are, recognize them wherever they go, imitate their dress, accept their slights, bow to their demands, and bail them out of trouble. Then we compound it by giving them millions of dollars for basically showing up and knowing their lines. Usually.

Is it any wonder that they are a little "different"? It's the *normal human response* to stardom. We don't let them off the hook, and why should they let us? It's amazing, under the circumstances, that any movie star approaches normality at all. The newly minted have the most trouble; those upon whom stardom is inflicted very early or very late in life often have an easier time adjusting.

A subspecies, seldom heard anymore, is the starlet. This term formerly conjured up a dewy-eyed, innocent young woman, struggling to make her mark in Hollywood. This charming concept has gone from quaint to extinct— sort of like the **casting couch,** with which it was usually associated.

Star Rule: Never, ever make a plan that depends on a movie star showing up on time for lunch, work, publicity stills, interviews, parties, or almost any other event. (This usually includes wardrobe, hair, makeup, and set calls.) Robert Redford holds the twentieth-century record for lateness: His personal best on-time record hovers somewhere around .027 percent. (Marilyn Monroe, Judy Garland, and W.C. Fields may have eclipsed him, but that was before records were kept.) There are exceptions to this rule, but the list is short.

Star Budget Rule: Anytime there's a "movie star" involved, add at least 10 percent to the normal costs and schedule. Working with a star necessarily entails spending extra time trying out bad ideas and also exciting ideas, extra takes, extra crew, excellent as well as occasionally preposterous instincts that need to be considered or tried, and finally, potential tantrums and self-indulgent behavior. It all comes with the territory, so why not accommodate it up front? Figure at least an hour a day. Call it star insurance.

star math The relationship of a star's ego to his/her talent.

Steadicam Invented by wizard Garrett Brown—who originally named it "The Brown Stabilizer"—this human-mounted camera revolutionized filmmaking. Virtually replacing the dolly, it allows the operator to travel with the camera in a way that had only been dreamed of before. (In the 1920s, F. W. Murnau—the legendary silent film director—fantasized about a camera that could "move freely in space . . . go anywhere at any speed" that would evolve "when the camera has at last been dematerialized.")

Half man/half steadicam

In 1976, *Bound for Glory* **D.P.** Haskell Wexler astounded viewers with a shot that cranes down on a migrant camp, then follows an actor as he walks through a crowd. The Steadicam operator was sitting on the end of the crane, then smoothly got off and continued the shot. That same year, in *Rocky,* the Steadicam followed Sylvester Stallone through the streets of Philadelphia, then up the steps of the Philadelphia Museum of Art. This shot, too, rocked the cinematography world.

The Steadicam has been responsible for most of the great **one-ers** of the last several decades.

studio The first movie studio was built in West Orange, New Jersey, around 1882. Designed by Thomas Edison's young assistant, William Dickson, it was basically a windowless tar paper and wood shack. It was nicknamed "The Black Maria"—alluding to the large black patrol wagons used by the New York Police Department. The studio itself was about twenty-five by thirty feet. The hinged roof could be opened and the whole shebang was mounted on a pivot so it could be rotated to follow the sun.

substantials In Canada, snacks served on the set. Also called *subs.*

suicide pin An adapter with two main ends.

sweeten To add a sound or music track to previously existing tracks.

> *"Courtesies of a small and trivial character are the ones which strike deepest in the grateful and appreciating heart."*
> —HENRY CLAY

A Few (Kind) Words on Setiquette

"MANNERS MAKYTH man," said William of Wykeham more than 650 years ago. Movie sets, contrary to their popular image, may be one of the last bastions of William's admonition.

It is fun and easy to portray movie sets as snake pits, full of strife, subterfuge, and hedonistic dressing room trysts. As the saying goes, "High school with money." But the truth is that sets are almost always models of civility. Perhaps there's something about having one's own language. Like the maritime and aeronautical cultures, the common language of the set binds its society together in a way that unites them to a common purpose: to get to their destination in a safe, orderly, disciplined manner.

Like a ship, a set has its own definition of time: The day starts when it needs to, not just when the sun comes up. Cut off from the rest of "civilization," day can be night; night can be day. The captain (director) sets the course; the bos'n (A.D.) rallies the crew; and the cook (craft services) tends to their appetites. A mutiny is unlikely but not unheard of: Unlike *The Bounty,* a set comes equipped with no lifeboats. Treated with the slightest of consideration, a movie crew will follow their director almost anywhere.

That's not to say that breaches of manners and morals don't happen. I've heard of fistfights and open warfare on sets, but over my forty-five years of working in one capacity or another in Hollywood, I've never seen them. The worst I've ever experienced is the sullen, unhappy, dragged-out unpleasantness of working with a rude or insensitive director, actor, or crewmember (usually a D.P. or A.D.). But nasty crewmembers don't last long; nasty directors (and actors), unfortunately, usually do. And from the personality of the director derives the personality of the set.

But this is also the true reward and power of directing: *You can force everyone to have a good time.* (It's good to be king.) A rude, despotic director makes everyone's life miserable for weeks and months on end, whereas a civilized, calm, and polite director can make all the hardships of filmmaking seem like fun. He also gets much more work out of the crew and cast. Some directors, of course, treat the crew like underlings; practically invisible in their servitude. Others—the best of them—are part of the crew. "Please," "thank you," and "excuse me" are part of their language.

It makes you wonder why such basic manners don't seem to permeate the rest of the industry, where the quotidian pressures, demands, and discomforts are so much less than they are on the set. But manners are a fading commodity these days. If I sound cranky about this, so be it; but if you want to distinguish yourself within the film industry, go to manners school. Learn how to write a thank-you note—by hand. Learn the value and impact of a small gift, preferably an imaginative one. Small gestures like these will set you so far apart from the rest of the crowd that you will never wonder why you are remembered the next time you call. Personally, I have a little cigar box of thank-you notes I've received from actors, directors, or executives for whom I've done a little favor or a good turn of some kind. You know: the kind of notes your mother made you write when you were a kid, thanking someone for a dinner or a birthday gift. I've saved them, so rare are they, wondering how many I'd end up with over the years. There are only a few, but you might guess who took the time to write most of them: It wasn't the "little people"—it was the stars, the big guns, the class acts. I don't even have to open the box to remember who they are.

And yet, there seems to be an assumption among many movie business executives, agents, managers, and lawyers that rudeness, arrogance, and bad manners are a sign of accomplishment. A ubiquitous disdain for punctuality is one of the more annoying and insulting habits. Another one is the lackadaisical—or nonexistent—sense of obligation to return phone calls, especially to pass on offers or scripts. Silence is the new "No, thanks." Most of these self-anointed swells have apparently trained their assistants in the fine art of superciliousness. Big mistake. Trust me, if you're looking to get into the movie business as someone's assistant, resist the temptation to acquire your boss's haughty attitude, or find another employer—a kinder, gentler one—before you take that job.

As for everyone else who wants to get ahead in the movie business—veteran or novice—you'll be amazed at how far simple courtesies can take you. So remember your manners.

Please.

T

tabletop In commercials, the genre of spots that deal with close-ups of products rather than live action.

taco cart A cart carrying grip equipment. Named after the ubiquitous southern California sidewalk vendors.

Taco Cart

talent People appearing on camera, usually only those with lines. Not necessarily talented.

tech scout To view a location with the heads of various departments (camera, sound, electrical, grip, transportation, and, of course, the director). For the first-time director, the tech scout experience is especially unnerving, as it will be the first time he wields the absolute, unspoken power and receives the respect automatically accorded his position in the crew hierarchy. The department heads follow him around all day.

television In the case of commercial networks, a medium existing with a single purpose: *to deliver the largest possible audience to the commercials.* While this, on the face of it, seems a harsh judgment, it is nonetheless a precise and accurate one. *NEVER FORGET IT.* Fortunately, this does not preclude some artists from doing original and important work. But the sword still hangs over one's head.

Television, according to the famous Ernie Kovacs quip, is a so-called medium "because it is neither rare nor well done." On film sets, the word is sometimes abbreviated and used disparagingly as "That's *so TV*," often by movie stars who feel they are slumming by doing television.

tilt An up or down movement of the camera on its own axis. Not to be confused with a **boom up.**

titles Usually used as a misnomer for the credits. The title sequence enumerates the credits: Director, Writer, Producer, etc. To eliminate the required credits at the beginning of a film and move them to end credits, they need to be unanimously approved by all the guilds involved. In that case, end credits must be comprehensive: No other credits may precede the film. Strictly speaking, titles would be separate cards on the screen, placed between scenes or sequences. The only true form of titles used today is subtitles.

The word *titles* originally defined chapter introductions to sequences, such as "Comes the dawn." After 1913, screen titles were written or made for the production, but prior to that they were made up in advance on stock rolls, which provided such items as "Wedding Bells," "Forgiven," "That Night," or "A Year Has Passed." The titles were then inserted where needed.

top To place a shadow across the top of something. *Top it down* is probably the most common and specific usage. (Also *hard top* and *soft top*, referring to the quality of shadow.) It is possible to request—and I have heard it—"Top it down up to her."

trailer A preview of coming attractions. Thus named because these were originally tacked on the end of the currently playing film, rather than the beginning, as they are today. (Perhaps a concerted effort could legislate that custom back into existence.) Often confused with the teaser, which is an abbreviated form of trailer, released well before the film debuts and before the trailer comes out, sometimes while the film is still shooting.

Trailers were originally text-only advertisements. The first trailer we would recognize as such, the "Animated Herald" or scene trailer, emerged around 1915. Paramount was the first studio to make trailers for its own films on separate reels that were shown before the main program. The year 1919 saw the formation of the National Screen Service, the now almost forgotten company that held a virtual monopoly on trailers and movie advertising for more than forty years.

No movie is ever better than its trailer.

transpo Shorthand for the transportation department.

treatment I'm including this even though it's not strictly a set term. I think it needs a definition because nobody seems to know what a treatment should be, how long it should be, or even *if* it should be.

Screenwriters are often asked to write treatments before submitting or even embarking on a screenplay. Here's my advice: *Never write a treatment unless you absolutely, positively have to.* In the first place, I've never read a great one; not a single one. Not even close. A great treatment is an oxymoron. It *can't* be great, because it's such a bastardized form. It's not a script. It doesn't (and shouldn't) contain dialogue or scenes. And it has to be short. So avoid them.

The problem is, treatments are very handy and welcomed (if not demanded) by producers because they provide a quick and convenient way to assess the finished or proposed script. Wait—there's a much more accurate way of putting this: *A treatment provides a producer with a quick and convenient way to say NO to your project.*

But if a treatment is absolutely unavoidable, just remember the *KISS* principle: **K**eep **I**t **S**imple, **S**tupid.

Just write a review of your movie as if you had seen it last night. Like a book review or a movie review without the critical analysis, it should make the reader want to see the real thing. Just say what the story is without all the details and embroidery. No dialogue, no flowery descriptions, no sales pitch. Just the *story:* Here's what happens, then that happens, then that, and so on. A page or two at the most. Write it well, but get on and get off. And always leave 'em wanting more. (That would be the script.)

While I'm at it: A synopsis is completely different from a treatment. It should be mercifully short; the most economical way you can think of to tell the story. Think of it this way: You're in an elevator; someone asks you what your script is about—you've gotta tell them before they get off twenty floors later. Less is always more.

trombone gobble Classic sound effect used when Warner Bros. cartoon characters are hit in the head. *"Whaah, whaaah, whaaaaaaaaaaah."*

trucking A lateral, sideways, traveling shot, usually on a dolly, right or left. Different from a **pan;** the depth of field is normally maintained as the camera moves past the objects.

Trumbull's Axiom "It's not the time it takes to take the takes that takes the time, it's the time it takes to talk between the takes that takes the time." Attributed to special effects designer and director Douglas Trumbull

(*Blade Runner, Close Encounters of the Third Kind, Silent Running, 2001: A Space Odyssey*). One of the great truisms of filmmaking.

turn over To start the camera rolling. Thus named for the days when the Mitchell camera had to be "turned over" with a rack-over device to ensure parallax-free framing and through-the-lens focusing. Still heard now and then, but "Rolling!" announces the same event.

turnaround The off-time hours guaranteed to actors and crewmembers between shooting days. A minimum time is guaranteed by the union agreements; stars often contract for more. See Haskell Wexler's very important documentary *Who Needs Sleep?* before quibbling or arguing about these limitations.

   The other type of turnaround occurs when a studio abandons a project and gives it back to its creators. Some of the best pictures each year are movies that have been put in turnaround.

turning around Reversing the camera direction, usually to shoot complementary coverage. Technically, not **moving on,** and a mistake to call it so. (*See also* **do-si-do, roundy-roundy.**)

twin buttes *See* **two Ts** (and note the pun on "twin beauts").

twin peaks *See* **two Ts.**

two-inch A 50 mm lens. Since 25 mm is almost 1 inch, lenses became known as a 1-inch (25 mm), 2-inch (50 mm), etc. Not heard much anymore, but "Slap on a two-inch" sounds unmistakably professional, and rather cool.

two-shot Two actors in the same shot. And remember, actors only, please. Calling for a two-shot of an actress and a horse would get the point across but would not sound quite right to the actress.

two Ts A shot framed from the chest up. It originally referred to the Grand Tetons of Wyoming. However, it seems impossible to think of it as other than "Two Tits." If you can listen to the *William Tell Overture* without thinking of the Lone Ranger, perhaps you can think of two Ts as snowcapped mountains, too. Can be, and is, used for male subjects as well as female, but the nuance is, of course, lost or wasted.

Two Ts

What the crew sees

What the camera sees

U

Ubangi A not-exactly PC word for a long, U-shaped plate used to offset or extend the camera from its normal mount. So named because it resembles the lip plate used by the African tribe.

under protest It was the custom, many years ago, for the **D.P.** to note that a scene was being shot "under protest" after being asked or ordered by the director to shoot it with insufficient light or in some other risky manner. This usually had the hoped-for effect of protecting the D.P. from the ax, lest the studio blame him for the results. The expression is relatively arcane these days, although sometimes invoked by script supervisors when **crossing the line** is in dispute. I once actually had an intractable actress shoot a simple scene "under protest" (her words), thereby providing the crew with the biggest unintended laugh of the entire shoot.

undercrank Since this nomenclature is counterintuitive, it's helpful to think for an extra nanosecond before using undercrank or overcrank. Normally, 35 mm film runs through the camera at twenty-four frames per second; it is always projected at that speed. Therefore, undercranking speeds things up; overcranking slows them down. A mistake here, at best, can be embarrassing; at worst, be careful what you ask for—you may get it.

Clearly the reference to cranking refers to the early days of the hand-turned camera. There was no technical reason for handcranked cameras; it simply gave the cameraman the choice of slowing or speeding the film in order to adjust the action to the audience. Silent movie–era cameramen were excellent at gauging when an audience would be bored by a scene or if the scene was moving too quickly, and would adjust their speed accordingly.

A cool insider's request or reference to undercranking is to "run some speed."

video village The encampment on the set, around the video monitor(s), defined by the chairs and the butts in them—the director, the producer, the director of photography, visiting executives, the director's guests, the producer's children, and anyone else of privilege who happens by. The use of video is embraced by many directors as an indispensable

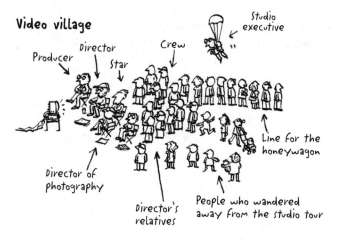

Video village

Producer

Director

Star

Crew

Studio executive

Director of photography

Director's relatives

People who wandered away from the studio tour

← Line for the honeywagon

tool and dismissed by others as a useless and time-consuming frill.

Every set has its own pecking order regarding the arrangement of seats around video. Once again, the director's *droit du seigneur* takes precedence. After that, it is often a tie between the **D.P.** and the producer and the **star**—usually subject to force of personality.

Historical Note: Video playback, which currently taps into the camera to display exactly what the camera sees, was actually "invented" before the invention of video playback. In the early 1960s, Jerry Lewis, who starred in and directed his own films at Paramount, attached a primitive video camera to the side of the Mitchell film camera. It was such a novelty that crews from neighboring stages would visit his set just to see it. (I was one of them.) The image was approximate, due to the parallax effect, but it worked . . . about as well then as now.

Warning: Martin Scorsese puts a mirror on top of the monitor so he can see who's standing behind him.

walk away A command to crewmembers to stop doing whatever it was you were doing, because we're going to shoot the scene whether you're finished or not. A polite way of saying "Thanks, but we don't need you anymore." Or, as in the game of hide-and-seek: "Ready or not, here we come." Assumes, usually correctly, that the **A.D.** is sufficiently omniscient to be sure that everything is in order.

walk-and-talk As the name implies, two, or sometimes more, actors walking and talking. A directorial no-brainer, as only two decisions need to be made here: 1) do it as a **one-er**? or 2) what is the **coverage**? Even when not indicated in the script, it's a great way to burn off a long dialogue scene in a hurry. (*The West Wing* might be said to have elevated this device to considerable heights: Every show had a couple of lengthy, complex walk-and-talks.)

It's hard to imagine a movie without a walk-and-talk or two or three. But it's actually a rather contrived device. Think about it: How many times in your own, real, life do you remember a really interesting or dramatic walk-and-talk?

walla The postproduction version of **rhubarb**—i.e., the sound of many voices cheering, chitchatting, gossiping: whatever enhancement the scene needs. Those extras you see jabbering behind Tom Cruise at the party, that classroom of students that just won't settle down, those kids playing in the background: they weren't allowed to make a sound on the set. Walla is the expression "put words in your mouth" realized.

Walla Group:

available for weddings, press conferences, and sporting events

Warner Bros. haircut A close-up framed just below the hat line. A virtually obsolete victim of the defunct Warner Bros. westerns. Sometimes referred to today, vestigially, as simply a *haircut* by camera crewmembers unaware of its origin.

"watch your back" Instead of saying "Excuse me" or "Get out of my way" or "You're standing in the wrong place," crewmembers use this expression. Its democratic use makes it suitable for addressing anyone—including movie stars, directors, producers, studio execs, etc.—without offense.

Unwritten Rule: Especially on location scouts, if there is a sidewalk, street, doorway, or staircase, discussions with the director and various department heads will invariably take place in the middle of it, prompting this inevitable announcement.

welding with light Overlighting.
(*See* **flamethrower.**)

Wendy light A lighting unit consisting of some 200 bulbs, mounted on a crane at heights of up to 150 feet. Developed by the great cinematographer David Watkin, whose nickname on the set was "Wendy." The unit creates the type of smooth shadows found in the **real world.**

"we're not shooting a release date" Usually a director's way of asking for more time or money, or justifying going over budget. Unfortunately, these days many times one *is* shooting a release date.

"we're on the wrong set" Just another, cuter way to say **"moving on."**

western reload A lickety-split reload of film before losing the sunlight; just in the nick of time, one hopes. Another charming reminder of the heyday of westerns.

wetdown Ever notice how the streets and sidewalks in a movie always seem to be wet, day or night? Probably not; but it's because they photograph so much better that way—and because the **D.P.** really, really wanted them to be like that. So the budget and the schedule allowed for a water truck and a wetdown.

wet print Inaccurately, but hyperbolically and colorfully, refers to a print hastily struck in conjunction with the first **preview** or the opening of the film. The image intended is that of rolls of film, freshly pulled from the soup at the **lab,** dripping with chemicals, being rushed to the theater before having had the chance to dry.

"what's your 20?" An expression used exclusively among young production assistants and assistant director–trainees while speaking on radios (always referred to as "walkies") meaning "Where are you?" Although a totally unnecessary code—derived from the ten-code of law enforcement and CB radio—it makes them feel part of the group. Also, 10-100 means you are going to the restroom; 10-4 means you understand, but "copy that" is cooler.

windbag Same as **butterfly.**

window In England and Canada, the last shot of the day, named long ago for the pay window where the crew would receive their money at the end of every day. Equivalent to the **martini.**

window "E" A 150 mm lens. Named for the registration window at the unemployment office where one would presumably end up if one were a camera assistant (focus-puller) who erred in focusing this very exacting piece of equipment.

workprint The first positive print made from the master negative.

wrangler The person in charge of a specific subgroup of crew or others. Traditionally, it was the cowboy in charge of the horses or cattle, but there are snake wranglers, dog wranglers—anyone in charge of some critter (usually) needing special attention. Even the person in charge of the babies on a set (these are almost always twins or triplets, due to rigid time constraints) is often informally referred to as a baby wrangler.

Wrangler

HEAD 'EM UP MOVE 'EM OUT

wrap Although it is usually the director's first impulse to scream "That's a wrap!" and abandon the set at a full gallop at the end of every shooting day, it is understood that normally the **A.D.** calls it. More tactful, then, is for the director to saunter off, or even hang around for a few moments after the wrap, as if he has plenty of energy in reserve and has actually enjoyed being there. A plausible, albeit fanciful, origin for this term (not unlike **M.O.S.**) is from an early notation on rolls of exposed film to "**W**ind **R**eel **A**nd **P**rocess."

writer "Schmucks with Underwoods," according to studio chief Jack Warner. The lure of easy money first drew writers into "writing for the pictures," although those short, silent films were not really "written." Frank Woods, the editor of a movie column for *The Dramatic Mirror*, was among the first and most famous of the "scenario writers" to come under this influence. In 1909 he sold three "suggestions" to Biograph for fifteen dollars each. He went on to write *Birth of a Nation*.

Traditionally, writers are not a part of the physical or linguistic lore of the set. Not really official crewmembers, they are often uninvited and sometimes barred from the set. Usually their visits are token and short-lived. They often have to fight to get their crew jackets at the wrap party—assuming they successfully lobbied to get invited to it in the first place. Many directors are either threatened (to put it bluntly) or intimidated by the feeling that someone is judging them while they work; although, inevitably, everyone actually *is* judging them, daily.

But the writer, the originator of the script, presents a paradox. On the one hand, he or she knows the script long and intimately, so who better to clarify or modify the script on the spot? On the other, he or she may have a very hard time letting go of their vision and accommodating someone else's.

Personally, I have a standing invitation for the writer to be there at all times, but there's a downside to that: *It's really, really boring.* Anyone who has ever visited a set without something specific to do will tell you that. So, given the chance to participate, most writers wear out their interest long before they wear out their welcome.

There is one universal, inviolable rule about having the writer on set: *The writer must never, ever, ever talk to the actors about the script, their performance, or anything pertaining to those subjects.* That means not even commenting on a "wonderful take" or a great line reading, etc. It means not telling a curious actor what a particular line "means" or "what they meant" when they wrote it. It's understandable: Nothing could be worse than for the writer to compliment an actor on "getting it just right," then having the director ask for another take—in a whole other direction.

There is no upside to breaking this rule; only the downside of humiliation, banishment, and—in some states—capital punishment. This rule also applies to producers, by the way, as well as all crewmembers. The only—and *very* rare—exception would be a specific dispensation from the director.

> *"Tact in audacity is knowing how far
> you can go without going too far."*
> —JEAN COCTEAU

The Writing Stuff

SO MUCH HAS BEEN and is continually being written about writing screenplays, that I hesitate to even comment on that art and craft. But I have such definite—one might even say dogmatic—views that I need to get them off my chest.

For the past thirty-five years or so (yikes!), I have been producing and directing feature films and cable movies. Almost all have been distinguished by a few things: 1) They were the first scripts ever written by their authors or their first scripts produced; 2) They were original screenplays; 3) The original author retained credit and, with only two exceptions, was the only writer credited.

Most of them didn't have agents, and all of the scripts were presented in unusual ways. But most important to me, for better or worse, was that each one was truly an original, not following in the footsteps of a previous, tried and tired genre or formula. That didn't necessarily make them easy to get made; on the other hand, I don't think it hurt.

So, I'm speaking here of original screenplays. Adaptations are a bit of a different animal and probably best left to the pros. But if you want to option a book or story and adapt it, go for it; other writers have done this with great success. Recent examples: *There Will Be Blood, Away from Her, Brokeback Mountain,* and *In the Bedroom.* No one hired these people to write these scripts. They all found a piece of material, went after it, and wrote their adaptations; no agent, studio, producer, or lessons required.

There's a quality that most first scripts share: fresh, surprising, and unspoiled. Recently, it was *Juno. Little Miss Sunshine* was a first-time script, as was *My Big Fat Greek Wedding. Good Will Hunting, Rocky, Sling Blade,* and *Taxi Driver* were all first scripts. So was *My Bodyguard.* None of these came out of a how-to book or a weekend seminar in screenwriting. First scripts usually come from a need to write something (or, sometimes, a *need* to eat and pay the rent). But with rare exceptions, they don't come out of a need to score big, to write a hit, to make a splash. And they don't follow in the footsteps of previous successes: They're invariably "surprises" flying in the face of what's considered commercial. Whatever their genres, they come from the heart.

Speaking of hearts: Tom Sierchio was a young, struggling writer from New Jersey living in L.A. and seeking his fortune as a screenwriter. He wrote script after script—six or seven in all—trying to write for the marketplace, trying different genres that he figured were commercial. No interest. Finally, in utter frustration and defeat, he decided to just write a script that he cared about—one from the heart. In fact, it was called *The Baboon Heart*. He didn't have an official agent, just a young junior agent who had agreed to read his stuff and represent him if he should ever get any interest in his work. The agent sent me three or four writing samples; Tom's script was one of them. It wasn't like the commercial scripts that agents are confident in. It was soft, romantic: a simple love story. My wife, Helen—an astute judge of writing talent—read it first and flipped out over it. I read it next and saw what she meant. We gave it to a studio on a Friday; they called on Monday to say they wanted to make it; a year later we finally did: She produced and I directed. It was ultimately called *Untamed Heart*.

Think you can write a good script? Then I'd say you shouldn't bother; good scripts are a dime a dozen and, as they say, "good isn't good enough." Write a terrific one, a great one, or you're wasting your time. There are thousands and thousands of scripts being written these days by people outside as well as inside the industry. Most of them are appalling; some of them are okay, some are good, and a few are really fine. Unfortunately, most writers are concerned with selling their scripts and therefore are seeking a way to do just that. I can't blame them. But I can't encourage them, either. Why? *Because you can't design a script to sell.* You sure can design a screenwriting *book* to sell though. *Throw 'em all out—off your shelf and out of your memory.*

Can you imagine a fine painter working today who's spent any time at all reading *How to Make Paintings that Sell*? Or a respected poet who's studying *Anyone Can Write a Great Poem*? And have you noticed any interviews with writers who claim they learned how to write their bestselling fiction by reading *How Popular Novels Are Constructed*?

The only true key to writing a really fine script is *talent*—which everyone seems to think they have, a lot of work, usually, and a bit of inspiration. People are readily willing to admit to their lack of musical, athletic, or drawing talent, but they're not usually so forthcoming about admitting to their lack of writing talent. I wonder why? I look at the number of screenplays that come at me from every angle: Internet, agents, friends, script contests, film schools, etc., and it's astounding to see how much time and labor is being frittered away on *really* bad screenplays. Everyone has a "great idea" for a movie—as if people ever walk out of a theater and say, "Wow, that was a great idea for a movie! I loved that idea!" Great ideas, commercial genres, and great opening scenes are a dime a dozen. Or less. It's the *execution* that matters; it's the *writing* that matters.

So here's my absolutely free "How to Write a Great Script" speech, book, and lecture series, all rolled into one: Get a hold of three or four terrific original scripts. You decide which ones. Read them; analyze them if you want, or just let them wash over you. Notice their format: it's standard in the industry, no exceptions. Then throw away or erase from memory all the books, articles, and lessons that reference or espouse three-act structures, five- and seven-act structures, "inciting events," "character arcs," "redemption," Joseph Campbell's name, plot graphs and charts, or supposed "tricks of the trade." Forget the mumbo jumbo and just write the damn script and finish it in 120 pages or less. If you're sufficiently talented, original, and inspired, *nothing else is necessary.* If you're not, *nothing else will help.* If it turns out that you lack one or all of those elements, write another script. Maybe another. Give up when you can't take it anymore. The time saved by not reading all those how-to books should be enough to carry you through the first several scripts at least, with time to spare. Sound cruel? Ask any screenwriter.

Those are all the positive, active things you need to know. Not easy, but simple. What *not* to do is even simpler. Years ago I made up a list that has, I have since learned, acquired a little life of its own among screenwriters. It's not about talent or inspiration: it's mechanical. Anyone can do it. I pass it along here-with. Ignore it at your peril.

My Dirty Dozen

These are twelve things not to do when sending a script out. Any one of them could make the difference between a script getting read, sold, or scrapped. I didn't really make up these rules: I just kind of real-ized or discovered them, like the laws of motion. Then I put them on paper:

1. Don't use a fancy cover.
The simpler the better. No zebra-skin motif; no artwork, hand-lettering, photos, or gimmicks. Make sure it is soft-bound cardstock or flexible plastic, not a hardcover notebook. The script should be on three-hole punched white paper (twenty-pound standard typing paper) bound with three heavy brads of adequate strength to hold it together when one gets halfway through, or "script screws" if you can find them.

2. Don't include a list of characters or their biographies.

The script has to stand on its own, and the characters have to be introduced so that it's clear who they are, how they're related, and whether they're the leads. It's not a play; it's a screenplay. There's a big difference.

3. Don't suggest casting.

It has become common practice in a pitch to mention that "Tiffany" could be played by Julia Roberts or a "Sandra Bullock type," but don't ever mention an actor's name in a screenplay.

4. The title page should be as simple as possible.

Centered: The Title. Beneath it: An Original Screenplay by Your Name. At the bottom right: address, and phone number or yours. Don't ever date a script unless it's already sold. Don't ever number a draft. Do not write "Registered WGA." (Anyone may register a script with the Writers Guild of America, so it's not necessary to advertise it. Anyway, it's automatically copyrighted by virtue of your having written it.) Paranoia almost always signifies the amateur.

5. Don't include a synopsis.

It encourages producers not to read your script. If they want it summarized with a script analysis, or covered, make them have their own people cover it.

6. Do not apologize in a cover letter.

No excuses for anything in the script from misspellings to length to plot holes. If it's not as good as it can possibly be, don't send it. Fix it. An apologetic cover letter will accompany your script straight into the shredder.

7. Don't include camera angles or other technical directions.

Those are the director's or editor's or D.P.'s jobs. No CLOSE SHOT, PAN, ZOOM IN, or any of the dozens of others you happen to know or have just read in this book, unless there is a rare occasion when it is absolutely necessary for a story point. In fact, the direction CUT TO is a waste of space on the page and generally a redundancy: How do you usually get from one scene to another if not by cutting to it? (Yeah, I know: dissolve, wipe, flip, fade, etc. Don't write any of them.) No references to other movies. And no music; especially no lyrics. That's why they invented composers and music supervisors.

8. Don't suggest actors' readings.

[Angrily], [Ironically], etc. Only do this if it is absolutely necessary—and it probably never is. Elmore Leonard has written dozens of great books without giving his characters many inflections other than "he said," or "she said." Most good actors hate to be told how to read a line and automatically go through and black out all the parenthetical suggestions without even reading them. Incidentally (and speaking of lists), you must read Elmore Leonard's *Ten Rules of Writing*—as brief and to the point as its title. He didn't intend it to be, but it's simply the best, most concise book on screenwriting there is. Fifteen minutes, tops. Read it twice.

9. It has to be the right length.

Don't ever submit a screenplay less than 100 pages or more than 140 pages in length. And don't cheat by using wide margins or changing font size. Screenplays are printed in Courier or Courier New fonts, size 12. Place one-inch margins top, right, and bottom. Place one- to two-inch margins on the left. The average film script runs 110 to 120 pages, which translates, almost without exception, into a minute of film per page of script. You can't fool us.

10. Don't leave a word misspelled.

With spell-check programs on most computers, it is easier to produce perfect, clean scripts. But you still have to read every word carefully. It's a safe bet that a script will be rejected if it has half a dozen typos or other errors in the first ten pages. If you don't care enough to make it clean, the rest of us don't waste time reading it. The same goes for grammar. No excuses here.

11. Don't number scenes.

Scene numbers are only for shooting scripts, not for reading scripts. They are for breaking down scripts for location and budget purposes and to schedule the shoot. It's wonderful if you've bought fancy software, but shut off the scene-numbering function.

12. Use a good-quality printer or high-quality copier.

Laser printing or its equivalent. If it's not crisp, clear, and clean, it's canned.

It's fine to make multiple submissions in Hollywood, but producers won't return a script without an SASE. Because it costs more to mail a script today, e-mail is the standard. And Hollywood appreciates confidence. So think positively and fire off your best and brightest work.

x copy An exact copy of any sound track.

yelling down Complaining to the wrong person (meaning an underling). Attributed to a response by the legendary sound mixer Buzz Knudsen, who, while being dressed down by a studio executive for a movie that

Yelling down

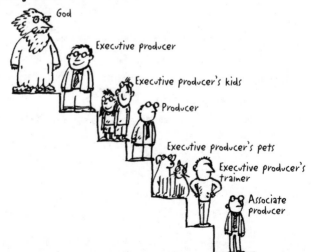

God

Executive producer

Executive producer's kids

Producer

Executive producer's pets

Executive producer's trainer

Associate producer

was going way over budget in postproduction, calmly replied, "Paul, you're yelling down. You should be yelling up." That is—in this situation, as in most others—you should be complaining to the director. It's often done by producers who lack the nerve to confront the director.

Yogi run Animation term for jumping up in the air and beginning to run before hitting the ground and taking off.

the zone The area near the particular city in which the (union) crew lives. A shooting area outside the studio zone is considered a distant location and requires different pay scales as well as lodging and/or travel reimbursement. The radius of the zone in Los Angeles is thirty miles from the intersection of Beverly and La Cienega boulevards. Hence the movie-gossip website TMZ (**T**hirty-**M**ile **Z**one).

Recommended Reading

Here are some essential books for filmmakers, written by people who know what they're talking about because they've done what they're talking about.

A Million and One Nights *by Terry Ramsaye*
If you're going to be a pilot, read about the Wright Brothers; if you're going to be a solo sailor, read Joshua Slocum; if you want to be in the movies, read this book. Like those others, it will tell you how these adventures began over a century ago, and what an impossible thrill it must have been.

Acting in Film *by Michael Caine*
Almost all an actor or director ever needs to learn from someone else about the subject. From a consummate pro who has been on more sets than most rental equipment.

Adventures in the Screen Trade
by William Goldman
Goldman's reputation as a screenwriter is open to discussion, but, as a smart and snarky inside observer of

the rest of the industry—mostly at the top of it—there's no one better.

The Conversations *by Michael Ondaatje*
Easily the most informative—and provocative—book available on the very fine art of editing. Perhaps this one should be listed as "required reading." Ondaatje and his collaborator, Walter Murch, take theory and experience as far as anyone has or probably ever will.

The Gross *by Peter Bart*
A year in the life of the business, written by the editor-in-chief of *Variety*. No one in the movie business is better connected than Bart. He goes way behind the scenes to ferret out the facts of the lives and deaths of movies and their makers after they leave the set. Pay attention; he's usually right.

Hello, He Lied *by Lynda Obst*
As successful producers go, she's "been there, done that." So, if you're an aspiring producer and want to be there and do that, too, you'd be well advised to borrow a page (or chapter) from her book.

I'll Be in My Trailer *by John Badham and Craig Modderno*
True tales of many people on many sets—really the only book of its kind. The subtitle says it all: The creative wars between actors and directors.

Making a Good Script Great *by Linda Seger*
"Good" isn't good enough . . . and if it ain't great, why bother? This is one of the few how-to books—among the hundreds out there—worth reading.

Making Movies *by Sidney Lumet*
Aptly titled, this is probably the best book ever written about directing. All aspects are touched upon and Lumet is, at 84, as good a writer as he is a director: a master. Nobody's done it longer.

On Directing Film *by David Mamet*
This is such a renegade point of view, and so thought-provoking, that it's worth a serious read. It's not a familiar approach; it's just a refreshing one.

Projections *by John Boorman and Walter Donahue (eds.)*
Since 1992, this (mostly) annual review has mixed anecdote, personal reflections, and comments from leading directors, editors, and actors on the practicalities of filmmaking. Reading any or all of these unique issues is worth the search on eBay and AbeBooks.com.

So You Want to Be a Producer
by Lawrence Turman
Well, do you, punk, do you? Then read this book. Like Sidney Lumet, Turman has been around long and successfully enough to speak ex cathedra about his profession. Take his advice.

Ten Rules of Writing by Elmore Leonard
In case you glossed over My Dirty Dozen (page 201)
earlier, Leonard's book is the single most sensible and
useful screenwriting book I know of. Although he doesn't
know that—he wrote it for novelists. It's so rigorous that
I've already broken several rules just writing this much
about it.

Visions of Light directed by Arnold Glassman,
Todd McCarthy, and Stuart Samuels
Okay, so it's not a book; so what? Why read about great
cinematography when you can, and need to, see it?
This wondrous film, like many of the D.P.s in it, won an
Academy Award. Deservedly so. Get the DVD; there's
nothing else like it.

What Just Happened? by Art Linson
Linson's an unusual combination of hip Hollywood
insider and tasteful maverick producer: a delightful and
effective combination. He's also a fine writer.

Acknowledgments

THIS BOOK WAS inspired by my wife, Helen Bartlett: my copilot in life and in filmmaking; in the air, and on the ground. Many years ago, she was the one who thought that it might be worth doing; I hope she was right. She never stopped believing in it, even when I did. Or, for that matter, believing in me . . . even when I did.

Everlasting gratitude to Jon Winokur, a *real* writer; author of many wonderful books, and a selfless and tireless advisor, to say nothing of his providing technical support in many times of crash-and-want-to-burn. This Doctor of Diction was always in and never too busy to make house calls.

Thanks to the kindness of two strangers: Mark Moskowitz and Jim Mustich. Their impeccable literary acumen and taste notwithstanding, they steered me toward my incredibly patient publisher.

And grateful credit to all the crewmembers on several continents who, over the decades, shared and let slip the secrets of their jobs, their language, and its origins. Especially to production wizard Phil Goldfarb, whose last-minute reading was my one and final litmus test.

Blessings and debt to the remarkable, ever cheerful and organized Karen Svobodny, who has kept our lives, our productions, and our studio running so smoothly all these years.

Thanks for the forbearance and support of Peter Workman, Suzie Bolotin, David Matt, and my literary life's first editors, Kylie Foxx McDonald and Michael Solomon; the support and friendship of Scott Berg; to Sonya Alexander for her research and initiative; and a tip of the hat to Ambrose Bierce who did this kind of thing first and better.

To Bud Yorkin and Norman Lear, who hired me onto my first set and treated me like I belonged there. And to John Calley, who gave me my first chance to go farther.

And thanks to just a few of those whose years of support and confidence in me has always bolstered, if not surpassed, my own; you might not know it, but you kept me going:

Bob Balaban, Kelly Bates, Mary Bill, John Bill, Joan Boorstein, Charley Carner, Francis Coppola, Christine Cuddy, Dean Devlin, Lise Fayolle, Jeffrey

Fiskin, Scott Frank, Bryan Gordon, Ulu Grosbard, Lynn Grossman, Axel Hubert, David Ladd, Martha Luttrell, Terry Malick, Mike Medavoy, Nick Meyer, Marcia Nasatir, Jessie Nelson, Jerry Offsay, Michael Phillips, Bill Robinson, Shane Salerno, Michael Siegel, Diane Sokolow, Sissy Spacek, Steven Spielberg, Jim Stein, Bill Tanner, Courtenay Valenti, David Ward, Dey Young.

I hope the colorful language of the movie set survives the digital age, just as I hope that the big, dark spaces in which strangers still gather will survive the home-theater age.

And—just so you don't take all this too seriously—remember what Jean-Luc Godard once said to John Boorman:

"You have to be young and foolish to make a film. If you know as much as we do, it's impossible."

In memory of my mentors:
Don Devlin, Stu Linder, and Sydney Pollack

About the Author

Tony Bill is an Oscar-winning producer *(The Sting, Hearts of the West, Going in Style)* and director of feature films *(My Bodyguard, Five Corners, Untamed Heart)* and television movies *(Truman Capote's "One Christmas," Oliver Twist, Harlan County War)*. He lives with his family in the oldest house in Venice, California. He has worked on over 100 movie sets and enjoyed almost every minute.

tony@movie-speak.com
www.movie-speak.com